PAPERMAKING

For my dad, Jon F. Kropper

Acknowledgements

Writing this, my first book, has been an adventure and it could not have been done without help. Andrew Buist, my husband, has been just wonderful from the start. Nancy Gray and Jon Kropper, my parents, helped by knowing I could write a book long before I did. Thanks also to Judy Buist who inspired me to begin papermaking.

The photographs on page 11; facing pages 16 and 17; pages 18, 19, 20, 21, 22, 24, 26 and 29; facing page 33; centre pages bottom left and right; pages 37 and 42; facing pages 48 and 49 and the back cover are by Michael Wroth. His ideas and patience were appreciated. The photographs on the front cover, the title page, and on pages 6, 8; facing page 32 and centre pages top left are by Geoff Hirst. Photographs on pages 15, 36, 40 and 41 are by Jean Kropper. Woodturning shown in the photographs on the back cover and facing page 33 is by Andrew Buist. Thanks to Lynn Oswald and Tony Pyrzakowski for their friendship and encouragement. Press in the centre on page 22, designed and built by John Buist. Moulds and deckles on page 11, kindly loaned to me by Geraldine Berkemeier of Primrose Park, Cremorne, NSW. And lastly, thanks to the Paper-makers of Victoria, especially Valda Quick, for all the support they have given me.

All the handmade paper artwork and examples of techniques photographed are by the author.

This 'Seahorse Fan' is made from recycled handmade paper with a linocut print, decorated with metallic inks and pastels.

LOTHIAN AUSTRALIAN *Craft* SERIES

PAPERMAKING

FROM RECYCLING TO ART

JEAN G. KROPPER

A Lothian Book

A Lothian Book
Thomas C. Lothian Pty Ltd
11 Munro Street, Port Melbourne, Victoria 3207

Kropper, Jean.
    Papermaking: from recycling to art.

    Includes index.
    ISBN 0 85091 505 8.

    1. Papermaking. 2. Paper, Handmade. I Title. (Series:
Lothian Australian craft series).

676.22

Cover and text design by Zoë Murphy
Illustrations by Tony Pyrzakowski
Edited by Janet Blagg
Typeset in Australia by Bookset
Printed by Colorcraft, Hong Kong

Contents

Introduction

With all the interest in conserving our planet's precious resources, there is growing interest in recycled and handmade papers. Papermaking gives us the opportunity to create unique stationery and art papers, unachievable by any other method, conserve our trees, and have fun at the same time. By writing this book I want to make it easy and enjoyable for others to achieve this satisfaction.

The basics of papermaking are fairly simple, yet the creative possibilities are endless. It is an ideal medium for people who want to try something creative without it being a struggle. You do not need any artistic training or even the ability to draw to be a fine papermaker.

Artists will also enjoy papermaking. Their training will enable them to see different possibilities in this extremely varied medium. It always surprises me to see another handmade paper artist's work, because it is invariably completely different from my own.

There are many parts to the long process of papermaking. I find everyone is drawn to a different part of it. Some people enjoy the methodical process of sheet forming, others the chemistry of making it last, building better equipment, collecting and preparing plants for plant fibre papers or creating artwork from paper. You will find your favourite part in the process after experimenting with it yourself.

I worked with commercial papers as a graphic designer for ten years here and in the United States. I was always curious to see the most exotic papers available. When I first saw handmade paper, I was intrigued by the unusual textures and colours. When I learned the basics and began to experiment, the satisfaction of creating my own papers and artwork had me hooked. Handmade paper art is a very textural, expressive medium. I hope you enjoy it as much as I do. Have fun!

Jean G. Kropper

'Reaching, Searching' is made from a monoprint, threads and leaves, embedded in handmade Abaca paper and decorated with inks.

The history of paper

Many materials have been used over the years as writing surfaces. Fifteen thousand years ago cave people drew sketches of their hunts on cave walls. Next, stone tablets were used. They were bulky to store and heavy to carry. Five thousand years ago the Sumerians began using clay tablets to write on with their picture alphabet. They wrote on them while the clay was wet and soft, then dried the tablets in the sun until they hardened. Wet clay was easier to write on than carving in stone. The Egyptians also wrote in clay tablets, but then found they could not produce enough for their needs, so about four thousand years ago they invented papyrus. They cut the stems of the papyrus reed into strips and laid them side by side. A second layer of strips was then laid crosswise on top of the first. Mud and paste was put on top and the layers were pressed until they fused together. Sheets of papyrus were born. Though its surface was still quite rough by our standards, it was a big step forward.

Two thousand years ago parchment was invented in the city of Pergamum because they could not get enough papyrus. Parchment is made from animal skins — calves, goats and sheep — with the hair and fat removed. It is stretched and softened. Parchment was light and easy to store, unlike clay tablets, and it could be folded, unlike papyrus. Though still expensive, it was by far the best writing surface yet, the first to be smooth enough for pens. Previously only brushes were used. Parchment is so good people still use it for some purposes today.

'Harmony from Diversity' is a collage of handmade papers, both recycled and plant fibre; dyed silk thread and a woodgrain relief print. Its theme is the bringing together of the diverse parts of ourselves and our lives to harmonise as a cohesive whole.

The Greeks and Romans covered wooden tablets with wax and wrote in the wax. This had the advantage of being reusable. Later they used Egyptian papyrus and parchment.

In 105 AD, in China, Ts'ai Lun experimented with boiling old silk and linen rags, tree bark, old fishing nets and hemp rope in water and wood ash. This began to break up the fibres. He then beat the fibres, breaking the mixture into a soft pulp. Next, the mixture was put into a large vat. He dipped a fabric-covered wood frame, the precursor of our mould and deckle, into the vat, lifting it up. The water drained off, leaving the pulp to dry on the fabric-covered frame. Ts'ai Lun had just made the first sheet of paper. Here, finally, was an inexpensive way to communicate and store information.

Paper became very popular in China and gradually spread to Korea and Japan by 350 AD. The Japanese did more experiments to find other plants suitable for papermaking. They found kozo, hemp, and later, gampi and mitsumata. Paper was recycled even then to conserve precious pulp.

In 751 AD some Chinese papermakers were captured and taken to Samarkand as prisoners of war. Their Arab captors learned about papermaking from them, then spread this knowledge to Egypt on their travels. The Egyptians experimented with this new process and added cotton to the list of usable fibres. Paper was cheaper to make than papyrus, so it became popular.

Papermaking did not reach Europe until 1150 when it was carried to Spain via trade around the Mediterranean. Papermills were started in Italy in 1275 and Germany by 1400. The first papermill in Britain was set up in 1490 in Hertfordshire, using linen rags, boiled and shredded for pulp. Papermaking reached North America with the Pilgrims in the 1690s.

In 1719, René de Réamur studied wasps and their nests. He noticed that the nests were made from wood digested in the wasps' mouths. Wood or complete trees had never been used for paper pulp before and he was curious. He experimented with various plants and realised that trees, in their entirety, could be used to make paper if they were broken down and treated properly. Since trees were bigger and much more available than old rags, the volume of pulp, and consequently the volume of paper that could be produced, jumped substantially. However, this volume of paper could not be produced by hand. The process needed to be mechanised.

The invention of the printing press in the 1400s created a need for even more paper at a low cost. Production of paper by hand was sped up but demand still could not be met.

In 1799, in France, Nicholas-Louis Robert invented the first papermaking machine. The invention was a real breakthrough, but he was not able to set up a successful papermill using it. His idea was taken up by two Englishmen, the Fourdrinier brothers, who set up a papermill with his machine at Frogmore in Hertfordshire. It was 1804. Their name has stuck, and many modern papermaking machines are still called Fourdriniers.

The machine consisted of a belt travelling through a large vat of pulp producing a continuous length of paper. It was pressed by rollers and cut into sheets. Finally, the growing need for paper could be met.

The mechanisation of papermaking soon put the highly skilled hand papermakers out of business. Inexpensive commercially produced paper was available everywhere. It wasn't until the 1970s that the craft was revived. Now there is growing interest in recycled paper, artwork made from paper and papermaking in general. People have realised that handmade paper has its own qualities that give it a special appeal.

Setting up

Most of the equipment you will need to make your own paper can be found among ordinary household items. The only tool specific to paper-making is the mould and deckle, and it is the most crucial piece of equipment, used to actually form the sheets of paper, so take care to get it right. Proper equipment makes everything easier. You can build your own mould and deckle quite simply, using basic carpentry skills, or buy it from one of the several suppliers listed in the resources section in the back of the book. A good A4 mould and deckle will cost between $70 and $140.

Here are a selection of moulds and deckles.

Top left: A3 mould and deckle of western red cedar with stainless steel screening.
Top centre: A home-made mould and deckle of aluminium using flyscreen.
Top right: A5 mould with deckle sitting separately on top. Notice the staples used to hold the screening onto the mould.
Bottom left: The back of an A4 deckle showing the rebate which keeps it in place on the mould and the back of the mould showing the horizontal ribs supporting the stainless steel screen.
Bottom right: The A4 mould, regular deckle and envelope deckle. These deckles have a pin that sits in a hole on the top of the mould to anchor it while in use.

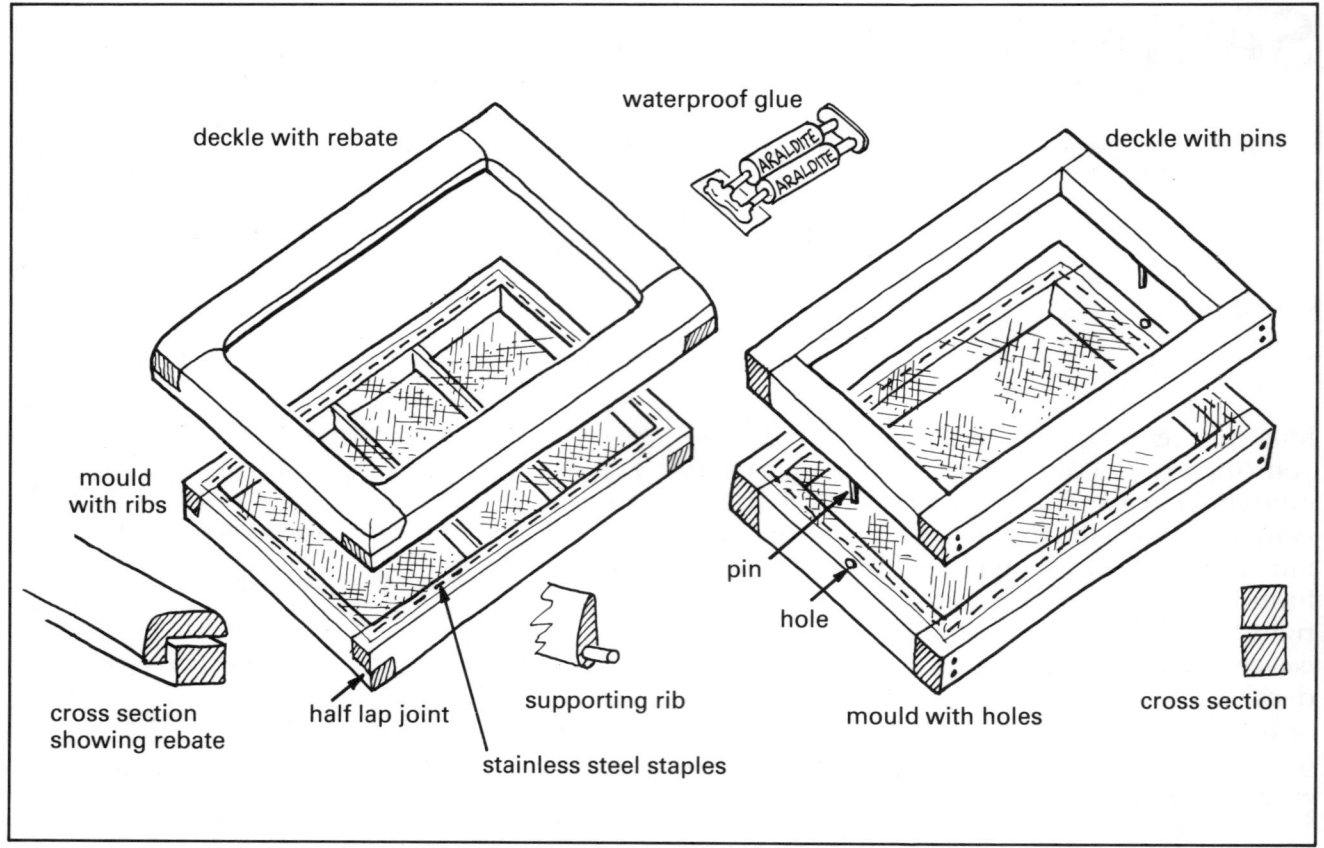

waterproof glue

deckle with rebate

deckle with pins

mould with ribs

cross section showing rebate

half lap joint

supporting rib

stainless steel staples

pin

hole

mould with holes

cross section

There are many ways of securing the mould and deckle. On the left is the rebate, where the deckle fits over the mould like a lid. The method on the right uses holes and pins.

The mould and deckle

The mould and deckle consist of two rectangular wooden frames of the same dimensions. The frames can be any size or shape. A4 (210 mm × 297 mm) or A5 (148 mm × 210 mm) are the best to start off with. These dimensions correspond to the *inside* dimensions of the mould and deckle. The deckle sits on top of the mould, and needs to be anchored there while in use, otherwise it is removable. The deckle may be simply held in place, or other methods can be used. It may have two pins through it, one in each end, that fit in holes in each end of the mould. It may have hooks on each end that connect with eyes in the ends of the mould, or it may have an

outside ridge or rebate that sits over the edge of the mould. The purpose of all of these is to hold the deckle in place over the mould. See diagrams and read step 7 on page 20 to understand how the mould and deckle is used. This will help these instructions make sense. All these methods work. Which you use is up to you. Your choice makes no difference to the quality of the paper.

Building a mould and deckle
The wooden frame of the mould is covered with screening. When making the mould, be sure the screening is stiff and stretched tight. Loose screening, often found on the cheaper bought mould and deckles, makes it much harder to transfer the paper from the mould to the wet blanket. A rigid flat surface of screening ensures even draining of water and an even thickness to the paper. The screening is ideally stainless steel, phosphor bronze or brass, held in place by stainless steel staples. The rough edges of the mesh are covered with glue, with copper or brass strips tacked in place or with a fabric tape glued down. Ordinary flyscreen or fine plastic mesh can be used on A4 or A5 moulds if it is stretched tight across the mould. Or, even better, use both

flyscreen and a coarser, more rigid metal mesh behind it to increase its rigidity and give it more support. This works for larger moulds as well. The top quality moulds have wooden ribs with tapered edges under the screening to give it that same supported surface.

Teak, western red cedar, or any hardwood will work for the mould and deckle. The wood needs to be durable even when wet frequently. The corners can be half lap joints or finger joints. Glue them with a waterproof glue: Araldite, Selleys 308, or Resourcinol, all available in hardware stores. The wood should then be sealed with two coats of polyurethane or Estapol. You can also use nickel-plated nails (these won't rust), but it is not really necessary. Look over the diagrams of ways to build mould and deckles, and the photographs on page 11, to see which is easiest for you. Remember, the most important thing is to build *a* mould and deckle and get started. You can always make improvements later.

Other equipment

Rubber gloves
Gloves are important when handling recycled paper pulp. Gloves protect your hands from the effects of being in water for a long time. They also protect you from lead and other harmful chemicals in printing inks which can be absorbed through the skin. So, wear them for your own protection!

Household blender
The blender is used to break up paper scraps into pulp. Always be sure the blender is clean to begin with and scrupulously clean after using it for paper. I suggest taking it apart and cleaning it piece by piece. Some printing inks have lead in them which is definitely *not* good for your health.

Never put your fingers into the blender: use a wooden spoon to free any pulp stuck to the sides. And remember, household blenders have small engines and are designed for food and not for pulping papers. Their motors are only strong enough to process a *small* handful of shredded paper, in a full container of water, at a time. Do *not* put more paper scraps in when you want to speed up the process. This will burn out your motor. Take a break when you feel impatient, then come back to it.

If you do not have a blender you can break up the paper by two other methods. Boil the paper scraps in a large pan of water for 20 minutes, stirring constantly, or use a paint stirrer on an electric drill in a bucket.

G clamps or press
G clamps are available from hardware stores, but check your garage first. You need two clamps, with gaps of at least 10 cm. A bookpress or other screw-type press will also work nicely. See the photographs on ways to press paper on page 22.

Two boards
You need two boards the same size, sealed with polyurethane, Estapol or enamel paint. Waterproof or marine ply are ideal. It is important that the boards are sealed, because they will be thoroughly soaked by wet paper; unsealed, they will warp quickly. They need to be comfortably larger than your mould and deckle in both directions, at least 300 mm × 390 mm for A4 sheets.

Deep basin or vat
Your vat must be comfortably larger than your mould and deckle. Plastic storage bins, styrofoam boxes (often found discarded behind seafood restaurants and fruit shops), baby's baths or washing tubs can all be used. Bring your mould and deckle with you when buying a vat to ensure it is large enough.

Foam
A piece of foam forms a springy base that aids removing the paper from the mould and deckle to the blankets. Any of the following may be used: two layers of carpet underlay foam (about 20 mm thick), a few layers of synthetic quilt wadding, or even a wet folded newspaper. I have used synthetic quilt wadding in my step by step shots in the next chapter. Whatever is used, it should be thoroughly soaked with water first.

Blankets
Also called 'wool felts' or 'felts', blankets are used to separate sheets of paper and draw water away from the paper during pressing. They are called 'felts' or 'blankets' regardless of what fabric you use — an old wool blanket, a cotton bedsheet, or sheer nylon mesh curtain. Cut the fabric up into rectangles, roughly 300 mm by 390 mm or a bit larger. You will need 10 to 12 such pieces to begin with. Old wool blankets can often be bought cheaply at second-hand shops. The texture of the fabric is impressed into the paper during pressing so a loosely woven

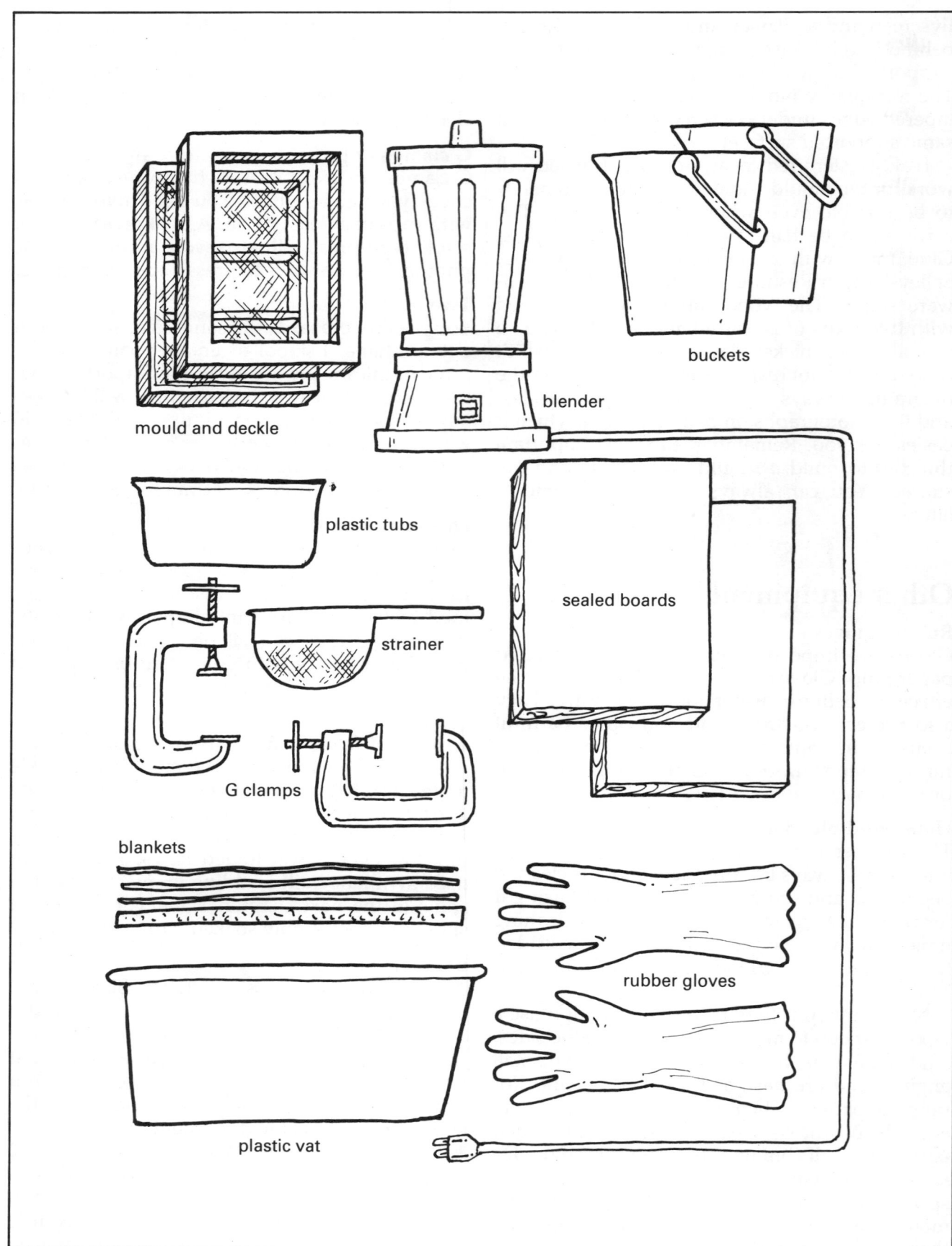

mould and deckle

blender

buckets

plastic tubs

strainer

sealed boards

G clamps

blankets

rubber gloves

plastic vat

Hanging paper to dry on a clothesline works wonderfully on sunny days with no wind. It is perfect for large groups.

wool blanket will produce a more roughly surfaced paper than a finely woven cotton. Each fabric works differently; experiment to find your preference.

Use wool or cotton 'blankets' if you are hanging your paper to dry on a clothesline. The paper will stick to them while drying, whereas it falls off nylon blankets.

Buckets and tubs
Use buckets and plastic icecream tubs for holding and transferring pulp and water between containers. Do not use glass as it is easy to drop bottles when your hands are wet.

Household strainer
Use a strainer to separate the pulp from the vat of pulp-and-water mixture when you stop at the end of the day. A larger strainer makes the job faster. Pulp can then be frozen and used another time. A large square of synthetic mesh fabric held across the top of a bucket can also be used.

You can assemble most of your equipment from items found around the house.

Paint roller or large soft brush
A roller or brush is helpful when transferring pressed paper from the blankets to glass or fibro sheets to dry. They are used to smooth the paper onto the drying surface.

Surfaces for drying paper
Paper can be dried on sheets of glass, on fibro (Hardi-Flex from a hardware store), on old printing plates, or it can be pegged on a line (see the photograph above). The choice depends on what is available to you, how much time you have, and how you intend to use the paper.

• Drying paper on a clothesline is quick and easy because no equipment is needed. However, the paper does not dry with as smooth a surface as when dried on glass. If you want a smooth surface, spray-mist the paper with water and iron it. Stacking it in a pile and pressing it under heavy books overnight will make it flat.

If it is windy the paper cannot be hung on the clothesline; it will be blown off the blankets and damaged before it has a chance to dry. Instead, leave it in the press and hang it when the wind dies down.

• Drying paper on glass gives the paper a very smooth surface, ideal for printmaking or calligraphy. It does take a full day to dry, however, so I prefer to dry my paper on fibro sheets. The water is absorbed into the fibro, which speeds drying to a few hours and the paper has a reasonably smooth surface which suits my purposes. Large sheets of fibro can be bought at a hardware store for under $20. This gives me enough room to dry 12 sheets of paper at once. Ask the salesperson to cut the sheets down to a manageable size for you.

• Drying time for any method depends on the weather and the thickness of your paper so times mentioned here are only approximate. The paper is dry when it falls off the drying surface or peels away easily.

'Mitre Shells' (top) and 'Nautilus' (bottom). Linocut prints in periwinkle blue on handmade recycled paper embedded with coloured threads.

The process of papermaking

In this chapter, the basic steps to forming your first sheets of handmade paper are described. Read this whole section, particularly 'Step by step from the beginning', before you start. The photographs on pages 18 and 19 can be referred to as an easy key to the process when you are up to your elbows in pulp! A glossary is provided at the end of the book to define unfamiliar terms.

Step by step from the beginning

The simplest paper to recycle is shredded photocopier or computer paper. Many offices, particularly legal firms or insurance companies, are happy to give you a rubbish bag full. If this is not available, then you can begin with full sheets of discarded paper. In the following chapter, 'Paper pulps', other forms of pulp are described, but I do recommend you begin with office paper.

1 Prepare the discarded paper
Start by ripping the paper into 'bite-sized' pieces. Since this is tedious and does take time, it is best done as you watch television, listen to music, or with friends to talk to at the same time. The smaller the pieces, the more time it will save you later. Making paper is not a quick process.

Next, place all the ripped or shredded paper in a bucket and pour water over it until it is completely saturated. Cover the bucket so no debris, dust or leaves get into it. Leave it to soak overnight if possible. The water will start the

An assortment of stationery made from handmade recycled paper.
Top: *Letter paper and two cards with embedded linocut, floral fabric and lace.*
Bottom: *Letter paper decorated with pulp painting in turquoise, letter paper with embedded lace on the edge, and a card with embedded fabric.*

paper breaking down into pulp. The paper can be left longer than this, but after a few days bacteria may begin to grow and rot your pulp. Obviously, this is not desirable! A tablespoon of Dettol should prevent this.

2 Assemble your equipment
This is a good time to start assembling your equipment. Find your mould and deckle or take this time to build one. Many of the other items you need you will already have around the house. Papermaking is wet and rather messy, so set yourself up to work in a place where that is not going to be a problem. A large, waist-high table in the back garden or in the garage is best. There you need not worry about the mess and it can be fun. Wear old shoes and old clothes.

3 Prepare the blankets
Fill a bucket with water and put the 'blankets' in, swirling them around until they are well soaked. Put the bucket on the table within easy reach and put on your rubber gloves to protect you from any chemicals in the inks of the paper.

4 Blend the pulp
After soaking, your paper needs to be pulped. Here we use the blender. Place a *small* handful of the soaked paper into the blender and fill it with water. It is *very* important not to put too much paper into the blender. Too much pulp will strain the motor and burn it out. Take your time! This *is* a slow process which needs patience.

Start with the blender on low speed, turning it off for a break after every 10 second burst, until the big chunks are chopped up and the motor stops labouring. Rest the motor again, then turn it up to medium and then to high. Notice how the sound of the motor changes as the paper is pulped. Be sure to give the blender regular breaks so the motor does not overheat. The longer you blend the pulp, the more even the

Step by step from the beginning

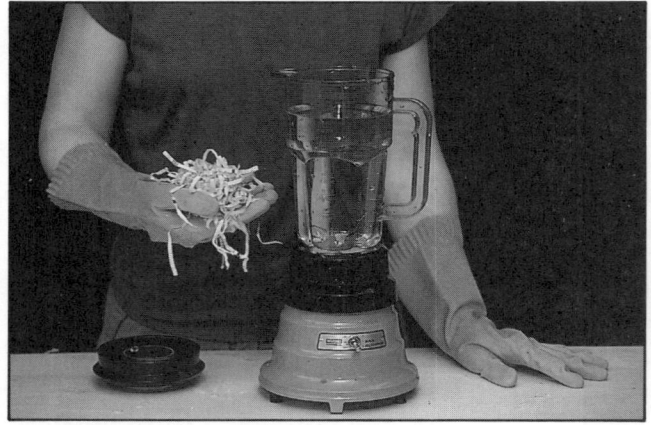

1 Blend a small handful of soaked shredded paper at a time in a full blender of water.

2 Pour the pulp into the vat until it is a third full. Add water until it is two-thirds full.

5 Lift the mould and deckle straight up, keeping it level, and allow the water to drain out.

6 Remove the deckle.

9 Lift off the mould, first one side, then the other, releasing the pulp onto the blanket.

10 Lay a new wet blanket across the sheet of pulp and smooth out any air bubbles.

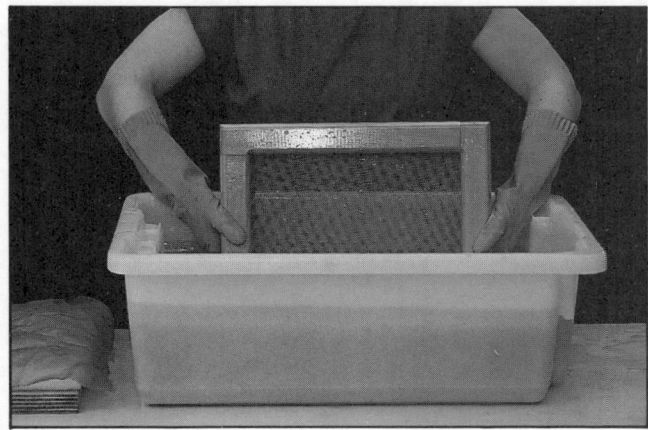

3 Stir the pulp then dip the mould and deckle vertically into the vat.

4 Turn the mould and deckle to a horizontal position and wait a moment for the pulp to settle.

7 Place the edge of the mould on your wet blanket and flip it over onto the blanket.

8 Rock the mould back and forth on the blanket using the heels of your hands. Press firmly.

11 Continue to form a post of 8 to 10 sheets. Cover the last sheet with a blanket and your second sealed board. Flip the post over, remove the top board and wet foam, and replace the board.

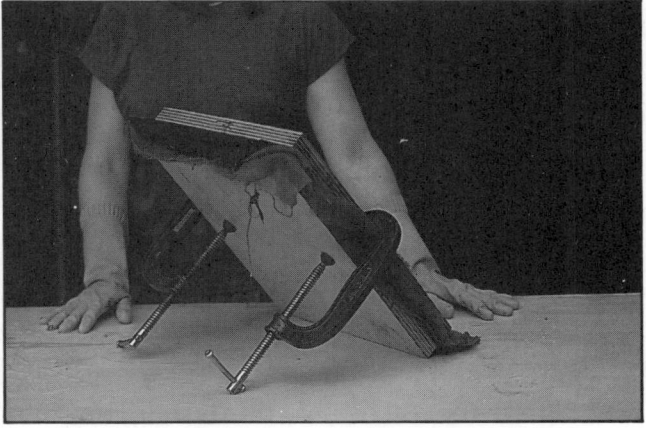

12 Position a G clamp on each side of the post and tighten. Sit the post on an angle to drain for an hour.

The ideal set up for making handmade paper is on a big table in the backyard or in the garage, where you can splash water and it doesn't matter. On the table from left to right: blankets soaking in a basin of water, G clamps used when pressing paper, post of paper, second board for pressing, mould and deckle, a bucket of extra pulp, large vat of pulp and water, a strainer and some lace for embossing.

colour of the paper will be. Shorter blending times will give a more speckled colouring. Do not worry about this at first, it will make sense after you have experimented for a while.

Watch that the blender's cord and the power point stay dry. Electricity and water do not mix. Clean up the work area as you go along so it does not get dangerously sloppy.

5 Pour pulp into vat

Pour the pulped paper and water mixture into the vat. Take another handful of ripped/shredded paper from your bucket and continue to pulp more of the soaked paper, handful by handful, until the vat is about a third full. Add water until the vat is two-thirds full. Use hot water in winter to make it more pleasant. *The pulp will feel much thinner than you expect.* Stir the pulp and water mixture before forming each

sheet. Keep a bucket of extra pulp nearby. Add a little pulp after forming every few sheets. Over time you will learn to adjust the thickness of the pulp to match the thickness of paper you desire. There are no set rules here: it simply depends on how you wish to use the paper. Experiment, and see what you prefer.

6 Prepare the post

The 'post' is the name for the stack of newly formed sheets you are about to produce. Place one of your sealed boards on the table. On top of that, put two sheets of foam or synthetic quilt wadding, well soaked in water. Yes, it will drip all over the table! Take one wet blanket and lay it across your wet quilt wadding or foam. Smooth out any wrinkles or air bubbles. This is the beginning of your 'post'.

7 Dip the mould and deckle

You are ready to make your first sheet of paper! Hold the mould and deckle together, in two hands, one at each end. Dip the mould and deckle vertically into the vat, then turn it horizontally under the water. Wait a few seconds for the pulp to settle, then lift the mould and deckle straight up in one quick movement, keeping it level. Holding the mould and deckle over the vat, shake it slightly from side to side, letting the water drain out of the pulp. The gentle shake helps strengthen the sheet by evenly distributing the fibres across the mould. Then hold the mould in one hand and lift off the deckle with the other, or get a friend to help. Be careful not to stick your thumbs into the pulp.

Put the deckle down; it is no longer needed for this sheet. The pulp should be 1–3 mm deep on the screen of the mould. If it is thicker than that, your paper will turn out like cardboard. Add half a bucket of water to the vat to thin it before forming your next sheet.

HINT: The mould can be used without the deckle when you want irregular edges to your paper. The mould used with the deckle produces a thicker paper with straight, even edges. The tendency to form thicker sheets is useful when your pulp is thin or drains too quickly. Another way of dealing with thin pulp is to couch two sheets on top of each other. They fuse together while being pressed.

8 Couching

Couching (pronounced **coo**-ching) is the process of transferring the newly formed sheet of paper from the mould onto the blanket.

Hold the mould with both hands again and flip it over onto the wet blanket, pulp side down. Rock the mould back and forth by pressing the heels of your hands alternately against the near and far edges of the mould. See the step by step photos on page 19 for clarification. Rocking makes the pulp stick to the wet blanket instead of the screen of the deckle. This process is called couching. Lift one edge, then the whole mould, off the blankets. Voilà! You have made your first sheet of paper.

Do not worry if the sheet did not come off the mould cleanly. Leave it. The first sheet is the most difficult to couch. Keep going. Just be sure the blankets are sopping wet and your foam or wadding is at least 20 mm thick.

A sheet of plant fibre paper. The irregular edges are produced when the mould is used without the deckle.

9 Form the post

Lay two wet blankets smoothly across the new sheet of paper, one at a time. Smooth out any air bubbles. You only need *one* blanket but, for the beginner, two blankets make it easier to separate the new sheets of paper without damage. Make another sheet of paper, couching it onto your blankets directly over the first. Continue this process, alternating paper and blankets, until you have a post of 8 to 10 sheets of paper.

Remember to add more pulp to the vat after every few sheets. This ensures that the thickness of the paper you are producing stays the same.

The blankets keep the sheets of paper separate and help draw the water away from the paper during pressing. Cover the last sheet of paper with a blanket and place your second board on top. Flip the whole post or 'sandwich' over, and lift off the other board. Remove the wet quilt wadding or foam, and replace the board. Now you are ready to press your paper.

10 Press the paper

Back at the beginning, I suggested you get out all your equipment. Take a look at the photograph above of ways to press paper. Choose which you will use. The pair of G clamps is the simplest

Here are three simple ways to press paper:
Left: Press paper between two boards of waterproof plywood using G clamps.
Centre: Build yourself a screw press using the screw and handle from an old vice. This one was built by John Buist.
Right: Use a small press with two large bolts and wing nuts through two sealed boards.

method. Have someone hold the post of paper while you put a G clamp on either side. Tighten as tight as you can. Water will spill out, so try to avoid wetting your shoes. Prop the post on an angle so the water drains out easily. By now you need a break, so have a cup of tea; you have earned it. When your tea is finished, tighten the G clamps a little more. Some of the water will have drained out, allowing you to do this. Leave the paper to press for a full hour altogether.

> **HINT:** Pressing the paper strengthens it by removing the water and allowing the fibres to begin bonding together. This process continues as the paper slowly dries. Paper that has not been pressed is never as strong as pressed paper.

22

11 Repeat the process

While your first post of paper is being pressed, you can decide if you want to make more sheets or stop now. If you want to continue, you will need more paper pulp. You will have used a lot of the pulp from the vat in your sheets. It will be thin by now. Go ahead and chop up more paper scraps in the blender and pour them into the vat. Do not add any extra water to the basin this time. You will learn to judge the thickness of the pulp as you go along. Continue as before.

12 Strain the pulp

When you want to stop, get out your strainer. Scoop out a small bucketful of the water and pulp mixture from the vat. Pour this through the strainer. This catches the pulp. When all the water has drained off, dump the pulp into a dry bucket. Keep going until all the water has been strained off and all you have left is a bucket of pulp. The pulp can be balled up and stored in a plastic bag in the refrigerator for a few days, or in the freezer long-term (be sure to label it).

When you are ready to finish for the day, pour the pulp and water mix through a strainer and save the pulp that remains.

Clean up all the drips of pulp in your work area while it is still wet. Dry pulp sticks to some surfaces and is difficult to remove. Rinse and dry your mould and deckle and store it safely; it is a precious piece of equipment.

13 Drying the paper

After your paper has been pressed for an hour or so, no more water should be draining out. Undo the G clamps and remove the top board. Now you need to decide how you want to dry your paper.

• **Drying on the clothesline:** If you are hanging your paper on the clothesline, carry your post of paper to a table or chair nearby. Carefully peel off the top blanket, starting at one corner, leaving the paper stuck to the next blanket underneath. Often the paper will be stuck between two blankets and will begin to rip if they are separated. Rub your hand, palm down flat, firmly across the top blanket a few times. This loosens the paper from the top blanket, allowing you to remove it, peeling it back from one corner. Peel up the next blanket, with the sheet of paper on it. Hang to dry, making sure the pegs do not touch the paper. Sometimes a sheet of paper will be stuck to both sides of a blanket. That is fine — just hang it up as it is.

Continue peeling apart all your sheets of paper and hanging them up on the clothesline. The paper is fragile at this point and is easily torn. It takes time to get comfortable handling it, so be patient with yourself. When the sheets of paper are dry they will easily peel off your blankets. Your paper is finished!

• **Drying flat:** If you plan to dry your paper on glass or fibro sheets, then get them out. Lean them against a wall, on your table or out on the grass. Go back to your post of paper and peel apart the blankets as above. Lay each blanket, paper side down, on the fibro or glass. Rub the back of the blanket with the flat palm of your hand or a paint roller to release the paper. Carefully peel up the blanket from one corner, leaving the paper. Smooth the paper down with the paint roller or a wide soft brush to give it a smoother surface. Leave to dry. Paper dries much faster on fibro than on glass, but does not have so smooth a surface.

14 Size

If you plan to paint or write on your papers you will want to size them first. See page 32 for instructions.

Taking paper out of the press to dry

1 Undo the G clamps and remove the top board.

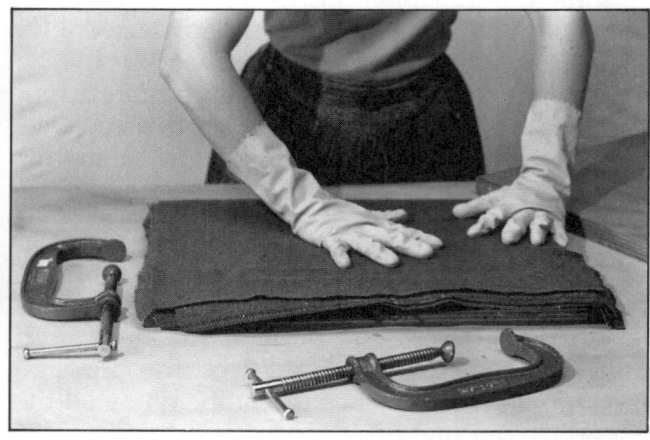

2 Rub your hand firmly across the top blanket a few times to loosen the paper.

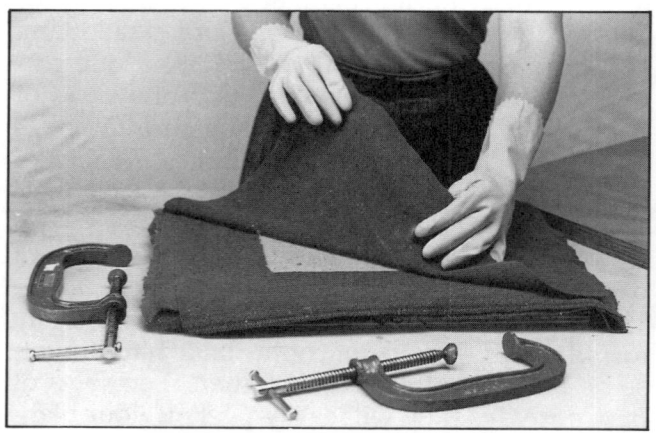

3 Starting at one corner, carefully peel off the top blanket. If the top sheet of paper is sticking to it, repeat step two.

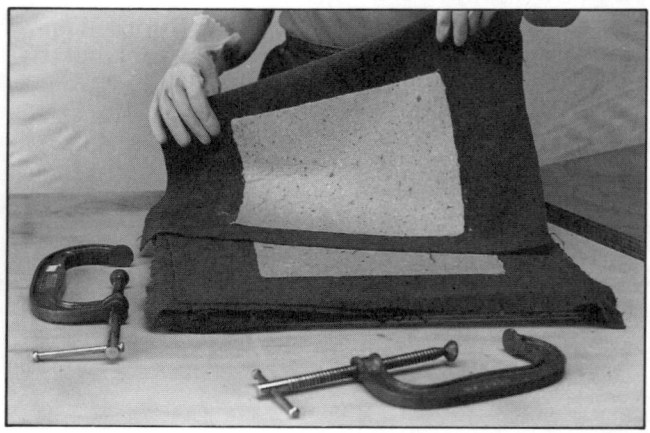

4 Starting at one corner and using both hands, lift up the second blanket with the paper stuck to it.

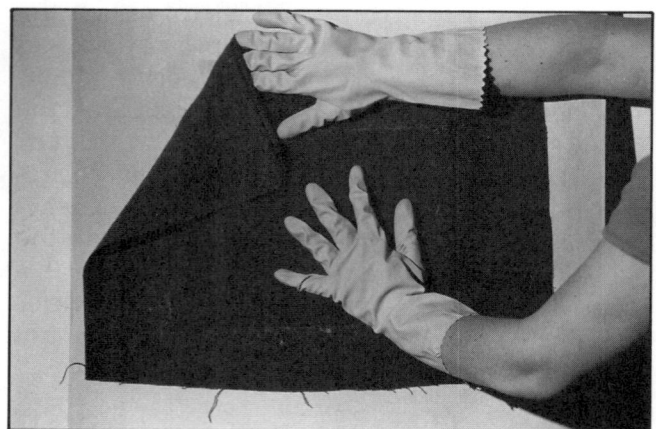

5 Place the blanket against the drying surface, paper side down, and rub the back of the blanket to loosen the paper and stick it to the drying surface.

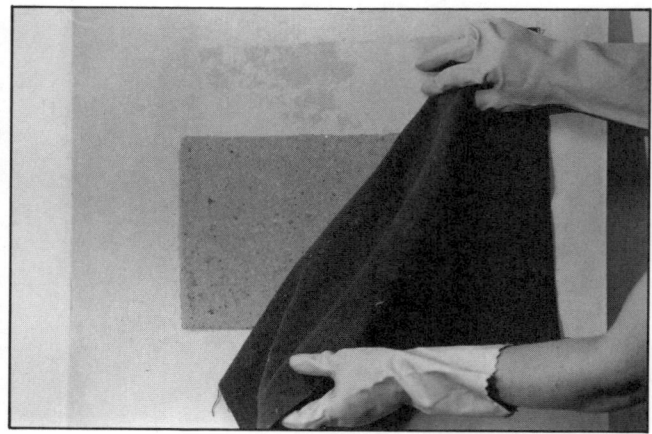

6 The paper will peel away easily when dry.

15 Cleaning up

After you are finished, there is still the cleaning up. Throw the blankets in the washing machine and the dryer. The dryer is very helpful because it pulls off all the bits of paper pulp stuck to the blankets. All you need to do is clean the pulp out of the lint filter! If you do not have a dryer, you will have to pick off the bits of pulp by hand. Otherwise, the pulp will stick to the next sheet of paper you make on that blanket. This is particularly annoying if your next sheet is a different colour.

Problem solving

Kissing it back

There is a simple technique to remove pulp from the mould if you make a mistake *before* couching. Remember, 'couching' is transferring your pulp from the mould to the blankets. Your pulp might be too thin, uneven, or have a thumbprint hole in it. To 'kiss it back', turn over your mould and deckle and lightly touch the pulp-covered screen of the mould to the surface of the water in the vat. The pulp will float off back into the water, leaving the mould clean and ready to be used again for your next sheet. Do not immerse the mould, or pulp will stick to the back of it and interfere with drainage.

If you make a mistake *after* couching the sheet, scoop up the pulp from the blanket with your hand. Rub the pulp between your fingers to break up any lumps as you drop it back in the vat. Then stir the pulp well to prevent any lumps in the next sheet.

Paper too stiff or thick

If your paper comes out stiff and thick like cardboard, then your pulp and water mixture in the vat is too thick. This is a common mistake for beginners. Add more water to the vat or dip the strainer in the vat to remove a few scoops of pulp. The thickness of your paper depends on how much pulp there is in the vat of water. Experiment with the pulp to water ratio. Paper can be made quite thin, thinner than you expect at first.

Lumps in the paper

If your paper is lumpy, the pulp was not blended enough. It may not have been left long enough in the blender, or you may have put too much pulp in the blender at one time. Go back to step 4 on page 17.

Difficulty transferring paper from mould to blanket

If you have problems getting the sheet to come off the mould onto the blankets, check that the blankets are well saturated with water and that you have sufficient padding (at least 20 mm thick) underneath the post. Then try dripping water onto the back of the mould while you rock it on the blankets, pressing firmly. Remember, *couching the first sheet is always the most difficult*, so do not despair. If couching always seems to be a problem, check if the screening on your mould is stretched tightly. If it is loose, couching will be difficult.

Circular marks

If your paper has circular marks or thin circular spots on it, the problem may be that bubbles are forming under the blanket or the paper when couching. To solve this is easy, so do not worry! First, make sure your blankets are well soaked in water. Second, smooth the blanket completely flat over each sheet of paper. Run your hand over the blanket so there are no wrinkles or air bubbles trapped underneath. When couching the next sheet, press more firmly on the back of the mould and deckle and rock it a few more times. This presses out the air bubbles and should solve the problem.

Paper pulps

Many different kinds of pulp can be used to make paper. Each pulp has its own properties: its speed and ease at draining through the screen of the mould and deckle, its opacity, its absorbency, its colour, how much it shrinks as it dries, how even or fibrous its surface texture is and how stiff or floppy a sheet is. Whatever pulp you start with, you will be amazed how different others are when you try them. Paper can be made from anything that contains cellulose: cotton or linen rags, wood chips, recycled papers and many different plants. Each produces a unique paper.

There is no 'bad' paper, only a bad use for a paper. A thick, textured paper would not be appropriate for stationery, but might be wonderful when used for artwork. When looking at the varied papers you use every day, think about the properties that make them right for their purpose. The cover of a paperback is heavy to protect its contents. Wrapping paper is opaque to hide the gift inside. Tracing paper is thin and translucent so you can trace through it. Paper towels are very absorbent. Each paper has certain qualities that match its use. As you gain experience, you will learn to adjust the qualities of the paper you make to suit your needs. When choosing a project, make sure the paper you make matches its intended use. Paper towels

Tea bags, envelopes, serviettes, newspapers. We use many different kinds of paper in our lives every day. Each kind of paper has different characteristics that match its use: opacity, weight, durability, colour, absorbency and stiffness.

would not work in place of tracing paper, and tracing paper would not work as wrapping paper. Think about the qualities the paper needs to have to suit your purpose.

All the projects in this book are designed to work with recycled paper, though many other pulps can be used.

Recycled paper

Shredded computer paper

Recycled paper from shredded computer or copier paper is the easiest pulp to find and work with for a beginner. It is top quality paper and usually available free for the asking from offices. Look it over before using and remove bits of plastic, staples or cardboard. None of these help your blender. I do *not* recommend recycling newspaper or egg cartons because they are poor quality paper. There is lead in newspaper ink, and the paper is very acidic and turns yellow with age. Handmade paper takes so much time to make, it seems sad to waste that time on poor quality pulp. Use computer or copier paper when available.

Sheet paper

Full sheets of paper need to be ripped up into 'bite-sized' pieces and soaked in a bucket of water overnight. Then continue in the same way as for shredded paper. A few sheets of coloured paper may be added for interest.

Cotton linters

Linters are an opaque, bright white pulp suitable to be used alone or mixed with plant fibres. They are not suitable for bookbinding papers because the fibres are comparatively short and consequently not very strong. Cotton linters have low shrinkage and are particularly suited for casting. They are available in sheet form from many art supplies shops.

Coated and uncoated papers

Basically there are two kinds of paper, coated and uncoated, and only uncoated paper is good for recycling. Glossy magazines with lots of colour photographs are printed on what is called coated paper. It has a layer of clay on it to make its surface completely smooth for colour printing. It is often shiny, and usually bright white. The clay in this kind of paper, and its heavy ink coverage, make it less than ideal for recycling. Instead look for uncoated paper. This may have some texture, and it is never glossy. Computer paper, copier paper, stationery and envelopes are all made from uncoated paper.

Choosing papers to recycle

Just about any paper can be recycled. Remember that the qualities of the original paper will determine the qualities of the finished handmade paper. Recycled copier paper will be strong and suitable for writing. Coloured serviettes, recycled by themselves, will be weak and very absorbent. Mixing the two will yield a versatile coloured paper. Keep this in mind when choosing your papers to recycle.

Paper for artists

Art paper can be made re-using failed drawings, prints or watercolours. It is good quality paper to begin with and can be recycled with delightful results. You do not have to remove paint. The inks and paints of the artwork give small flecks of colour to the recycled paper. You are not recreating the paper you began with, rather, you are creating something new. To me, the flecks of colour add interest, making your paper completely different from any you can buy. This makes all the work involved worthwhile. Artists concerned about whether handmade paper artwork will last should always begin with acid-free paper. Leftover scraps of acid-free mount board from picture framers can also be recycled. This needs to be soaked for two days to soften it before pulping in the blender. The coloured paper layer on the mount board is removed during soaking and before blending.

If your handmade paper is to be used for printmaking it should be lightly sized in the vat or left unsized. For watercolour, it needs to be heavily sized. Do not soak paper before printing or it will disintegrate. Instead, spray-mist it with water or dampen the pages of an old newspaper and place your paper between the pages for twenty minutes before use. Also, consider the character of your handmade paper and how it suits the subject of your print. An etching with lots of fine line work will not suit a speckled, rough-surfaced paper. Remember, the longer the recycled pulp is left in the blender, the more even its colour.

Plant fibre papers

Paper is made mostly of cellulose. Plants contain cellulose. Consequently many plants, when properly treated, can be made into paper. Plant fibre papers are amazingly varied in looks and textures. To prepare them for papermaking, the plants need to be chopped, retted (kept moist and allowed to rot in the open air), cooked, beaten and pulped — quite involved for a beginner. However, the plants in your backyard are free and it is an amazing process.

I find plant fibre papers fascinating. Each plant makes a paper with a different colour, texture, translucency and stiffness. Plant fibre papers are usually very textured, perfect for artwork. Alone, they are generally not usable for stationery. However, when combined with recycled paper, cotton linters, or recycled mount board they make very distinctive and versatile papers.

Bast fibres

There are basically three kinds of plant fibres: bast fibres, or the sap-carrying inner bark, leaf fibres and grasses. Bast fibres are very long and make strong translucent papers. Start by cutting branches 15–25 millimetres in diameter and 1–2 metres in length. It is best to harvest these branches when pruning to lessen damage to the plant. To remove the bark from the branches when green, slice through the bark with a knife and peel it off in strips. You will then have both the inner and outer bark, which need to be separated. Either soak the strips and peel off the outer bark, or scrape off the outer bark with a knife or potato peeler. What remains is the inner bark or bast fibre which is now ready for cooking.

If the plant is dry you will be unable to peel off the bark. Instead, cut the branches in 20-centimetre lengths and tie them in a bunch, as you would asparagus. Place them in a saucepan with two centimetres of water, cover and steam them for half an hour to an hour. Let them cool. Now you should be able to peel back the bark without any trouble. Privet, hibiscus, acacia, wisteria, willow, flax, okra, fig, gampi, kozo, mitsumata, mulberry and eucalyptus all yield

A selection of plant fibre papers.

bast fibres. When using a plant cultivated for its flowers, such as hibiscus or wisteria, harvest it after the flowers have faded.

Leaf fibres
Next come leaf fibres, which are shorter but more readily available. They tend to make opaque papers with a rougher texture: Canna lily, banana, birds nest fern, raffia, manila hemp, sisal, yucca, pandanus, strelitzia, iris, New Zealand flax, *Monstera deliciosa* and pineapple tops are all leaf fibres. Pick the largest leaves, since they have the longest fibres. Many of these leaves have a tough outer layer that needs to be scraped off with a knife or a seashell before cooking. Then they can be cut up in a garden muncher, or with secateurs or scissors, and cooked as described below.

Grass fibres
Grass fibres form the third group. Their fibres are short and tend to be brittle, but these plants are everywhere. They can be mixed with other fibres or sized to improve their strength if needed. Bladey grass, summer grass, pampas grass, kangaroo grass, young bamboo, cornstalks and husks, beach grass, bulrushes, papyrus, sugar cane and wheat have been tried. Discard the seeds, they will create lumps. When you are using a plant that is cultivated and harvested, such as wheat or sugar cane, collect the fibre after the crop is harvested. Some of these plants — bamboo for example — float in water and are awkward to cook. Split the fibres and beat them lightly first to stop them floating and then cook as described below.

How to prepare plant fibres
Plant fibre paper preparation is an imprecise science, which is part of its fascination. The time of year the plants are harvested, the soil they grow in, and the climate that year can all change the properties of the plants. Just how strong to make a caustic solution and just how long the plants need to be boiled also varies. Your own experimentation will give the answers.

1 Collect the plants, and cut them into 2-centimetre lengths using scissors or secateurs. You can try any plants, but some work better than others. Keep each plant separate in a synthetic mesh bag (old curtains are perfect for this). If the plant is very woody, like bamboo, it may need to be broken down further. It can be cut, dampened, and left in an open container to ret, which chemically breaks down the fibre; or, after cooking, it can be pounded with a wooden mallet, which physically breaks down the fibre.

2 The next step is cooking the plant material in caustic soda. This removes the parts of the plant that are not wanted for making paper: waxes, starch, lignin and sugars. You will need rubber gloves, apron and eye protection while doing this. Caustics will burn exposed skin and must be treated with respect. If you do get caustic on your skin, immediately flush the area liberally with water and see a doctor. Work outside or somewhere with excellent ventilation as the fumes are toxic. An old copper is ideal for cooking, or a large pot on a barbecue in the back yard. The pot must be made of stainless steel, copper or enamel (no cracks). Never use aluminium because caustic eats it.

3 Boil the plant lengths in a mild caustic soda solution. In general, plant fibres will break down when boiled for two hours in 10 g of caustic soda per one litre of water. Too strong a solution will make the fibre brittle. It is better to use a weaker solution and cook the fibre longer than to use too strong a solution. A more precise recipe is 18 g of caustic soda per 100 g of dry plant fibre. Always add caustic to water, not the other way around.

4 Next, wash the fibres thoroughly to get rid of the caustic. Use lots of water and continue washing until the water drains clear. If you wish to have acid free paper for artwork, test the Ph of the water coming off the fibre with Ph strips from a chemist or a kit from a pool or aquarium supplier. It should be close to 7 or neutral.

5 Most plant fibres will not break down completely in cooking and will need to be beaten. Place the damp fibres on a hard surface and beat them with a wooden mallet or club to further separate them. When they are ready they will spread in a glass of water without clumps and appear as individual fibres, whereas paper made from unbeaten fibres will be stringy and textured. Now your plant fibre pulp is ready to be formed into sheets of paper, as described in the previous chapter.

Keeping records of your experiments

When you experiment with plant fibres it is important to keep a record of how the fibres were prepared and of the results. This allows you to repeat your successes and to change the preparation method for fibres that did not work so well. For each fibre have one page of notes and one sample of the paper you made. A notebook with clear plastic sleeves is ideal. Include the following on your page of notes:

- Common and botanical name of the plant.
- The time of year the plant was picked.
- Was it green or dried? Did you ret it?
- The part of the plant used: inner bark, leaves, stems.
- The strength of the caustic solution.
- How long the fibre was cooked.
- How long the fibre was washed.
- How long the fibre was beaten.
- Was beating done by hand or in the blender?
- 'Freeness' — or how fast the pulp drained on the mould.
- Formation aid used, if any.
- How difficult or easy it was to form sheets and notes on technique.
- Drying method and amount of shrinkage.
- The properties of the finished paper; for example colour, translucency.
- Texture: is it even or stringy? How strong is it?
- Your ideas for the best use of this paper.

Bleaching plant fibre

If you wish to bleach plant fibres for a lighter coloured paper, try leaving the fibre out in the sun. A second method is to mix up a bucket of hydrogen peroxide and water and add your plant fibre to it. Stir well and cover the bucket to keep out dust and spiders. Let it sit for a week. Rinse off the fibre and record the results. This will not damage the strength of the fibre in any way.

Do not use chlorine bleach if you want your paper to be long lasting. Bleach does work quickly but it weakens the fibre and, over time, the paper will turn yellow and brittle like old newspaper. Hydrogen peroxide is the better choice.

Prepared plant fibres

If all the above seems like too much work, prepared plant fibre pulps can be bought to make things easier. The pulps are sold in thick sheets, looking a bit like mottled blotting paper.

Each bought 'sheet' makes many sheets of paper. The 'sheets' are soaked in hot water for a few hours until soft, then put through the blender in small handfuls like recycled paper. These pulps need very little blending, only enough to separate the fibres. Sometimes the pulps have dried out during shipping and will need to be boiled in water (no caustic!) for fifteen minutes to rehydrate them. The pulp is then formed into sheets in the same way as recycled pulp. Never cut these prepared sheets because you will cut and shorten the fibres; tear them if you want to use only part of the sheet.

The most common prepared plant fibre pulps are abaca, acabab, cogon, flax, suksuka, talang and tikem. Pulped plant fibre papers can be bought from One Stop Art Supplies in Victoria or Carriage House Paper in the United States. Addresses are in the Resources section at the end of this book.

Formation aid (mucilage)

Also called mucilage, formation aid is a gluey preparation made from plants. Some plant fibre pulps drain so fast on the mould and deckle it can be hard to distribute the pulp and form sheets with them. You may end up with clumps of pulp and areas of no pulp. Formation aid or mucilage helps solve this problem. Added to the vat, it thickens the water and pulp mixture, causing it to drain more slowly. Note that formation aid will only work with cold water in the vat.

Formation aid can be bought or you can make it yourself from okra root and vegetable, or prickly pear cactus. The process is the same. Be careful when handling prickly pear! Wear thick gloves, and handle it through several layers of fabric or newspaper. I hold it still with a barbecue fork.

Cut up several pieces of the plant fairly small, beat or pound them a little to expose the insides, and place in the bottom of a bucket. Pour cold water over the plant pieces to cover them. Leave it to sit for a few hours. Stick in a fork and lift it up to test if it is 'done'. The liquid will be viscous, like egg white, when ready to use.

Strain the liquid to remove any impurities. How much you need depends on the strength of the solution of formation aid and the size of the vat.

To begin, pour 150 mL into the vat of pulp and water. Form a sheet of paper to test it. If needed, add another 100 mL and test again. The fibres should spread out more evenly on the screen of the mould when the mixture is right. Pour another

kettle of boiling water on the plant pieces if you need more. Discard the plants when done. The formation aid loses its potency if stored, so try to make up only as much as you need. The plant pieces, however, may be kept in the refrigerator or freezer for some time, ready to be prepared when needed.

31

Sizing

Sizing makes the paper less absorbent and strengthens it. Sizing is necessary if you plan to write or paint on your paper, since inks and paint will bleed into unsized paper. Sizing can be added to the pulp in the vat (internal size) or painted onto dry, finished sheets of paper (external size). Painting it on allows you to decide, after making the paper, how you want to use it.

There are a few different kinds of size: animal (rabbit skin glue), synthetic (Hercon), and vegetable (corn flour, rice flour and methyl cellulose). Methyl cellulose (wallpaper paste) is readily available from hardware stores. It can be bought as 'Polycell' in small packets. Follow the directions on the packet, then dilute with more warm water, add to the vat and stir thoroughly. A strong solution of methyl cellulose will make your paper stiff and shiny, as well as adding strength.

Instant starch, in powder form from the supermarket, can also be used. This needs no preparation. It does not need warm water and can be sprinkled directly into the vat. Stir the vat regularly so the starch does not sink to the bottom or form lumps.

Make your own size

You can also make your own size. Mix 50 mL of corn flour or rice flour and 350 mL of cold water in a large bowl until there are no lumps. Put it in the microwave for four to five minutes, stopping *every* minute to stir it. Let cool. It is important that there are no lumps as this creates lumps and holes in the paper. Pour 100 mL of the mixture into the vat and stir thoroughly. Save the rest for next time. It may be stored in sealed jars in the refrigerator.

For methyl cellulose, corn flour or rice flour sizing to stay dissolved, the water in the vat needs to be warm. So add some hot water to the vat or blender instead of the usual cold water.

Do not pour size into the blender because it may foam up.

Sizing finished sheets of paper

Your sheets of paper should be left to dry completely for at least two weeks. Mix up some size and water, and simply paint it on your finished papers with a wide soft brush. This is perfect for calligraphy papers. Experiment, you may need more than one coat.

Note that vat (internal) sizing will soak into your blankets. Wash them thoroughly when finished.

Opposite: 'Tribal Song' by the author. Linocut, threads, and gold paper laminated in handmade Abaca and plant-fibre papers, with feathers. Inspired by a trip to the highlands of Papua New Guinea.

Centre opening left: 'Moving, Flowing' (top) by the author. Embossed fan made from recycled paper decorated with metallic inks and pastels.
'Kakadu Flower' (bottom) by the author, made from a hand painted linocut laminated in handmade Abaca paper and painted with inks.

Centre opening right: This is a selection of handmade embossed papers, decorated with pastels to highlight the texture. Look closely. Can you work out what was used to emboss each of them?

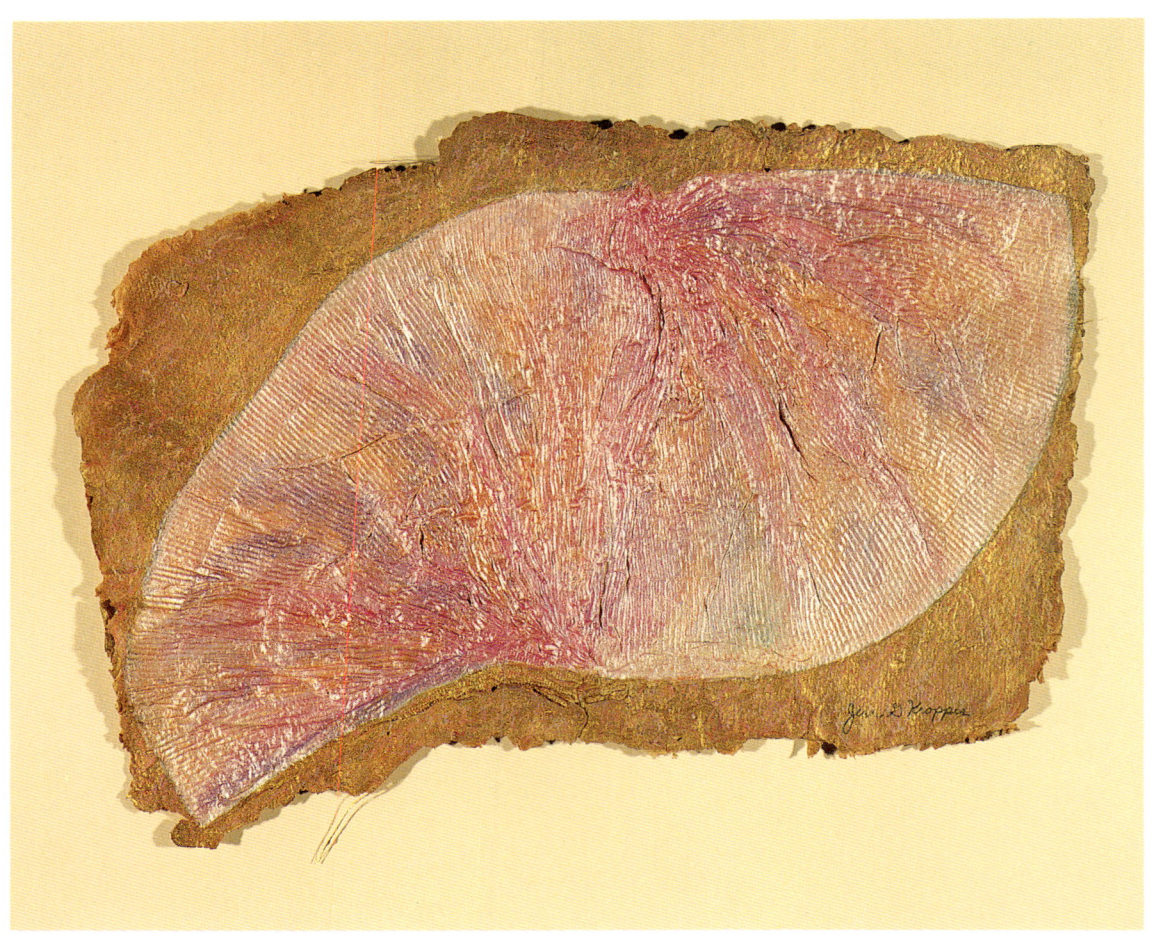

Variations

Embedding

Embedding means adding various things to the paper pulp so that they become part of the paper, randomly mixed through the sheet. Metallic and coloured cotton threads are easy and effective; they can be short, or long curling threads. See the handbound books in the colour photo opposite and the two shell prints facing page 16 as examples. Add the cut lengths of thread to the full vat of pulped paper and stir. Never add them to pulp in the blender because they will twist tightly around the blades, jamming them.

Confetti, old artwork cut into tiny squares, lengths of yarn and dried flowers can be added. Pour them into the vat of paper pulp and away you go! Commercially dried flowers are often dyed, and the colours may bleed into the paper. Some people like this effect, some do not.

Before being added to the pulp, flowers should be pressed between absorbent papers until completely dry. This prevents them from turning brown and rotting in your paper. Everlastings or paper daisies, pansies, cornflowers, rose petals, bougainvillea and royal pelargoniums or geraniums work well. They can be added to the vat or placed on a newly formed sheet on the mould. Leaves can also be added, but should be dried and sealed on both sides with PVA glue first.

Laminating

Images, photos, lace or bits of fabric can also be laminated between two sheets of paper. The images should be made with oil-based paints or be thoroughly sealed first. Water-based paints or inks will simply bleed away in the water, creating a disappointing mess.

Couch a sheet of paper on the blankets as usual. Place your image on the sheet face up, where you want it. You may circle it with threads or add scraps of coloured papers around it. Next, make a second sheet of paper that is thinner than the first. Do this by making a shallow dip of the mould and deckle in the vat. Couch the second sheet directly on top of the first, temporarily covering the image. Cover with another blanket and press the paper. After pressing the paper, carefully peel and rub away the paper pulp covering the part of the image you want to expose. Leave some pulp covering the edges to hold it in place. Dry the paper as usual and paint as you wish. See 'Kakadu flower' in the centre spread of colour pages, or the photograph of stationery facing page 17, for examples of this process.

If you choose to embed photos be sure you have the negative and can replace them. Water may damage the print, so do not use anything precious. If what you are embedding is large, brush a thin coat of paper paste on the back of it to help hold it in place.

You can make all these projects from your own handmade recycled paper. See the projects section for instructions.
Top centre: *Embossed card decorated with pastels.*

Top right: *Wallet folder showing the ribbons and button closing.*

Left: *Two small handbound books whose covers are embedded with coloured threads.*

Lower left: *Elegant folded fan necklace and matching earrings.*

Lower right in bowl: *Striped brooches and earrings, decorated with ribbon and strips of your own papers.*

Large, small and shaped sheets

Small sheets

To make smaller or differently shaped sheets of paper, mask the screening of the mould with tape or contact paper, leaving the area you want uncovered. Masking or packing tape work well. Rub the tape down with a fingernail to ensure it is secure. This can also be done by cutting into the middle of an A4 sheet of stiff plastic or X-ray film and placing this on your mould. Put your deckle on top of both to anchor the plastic sheet in place and form sheets as usual. You can make your own envelope deckle using this method.

Large sheets

You can make sheets of paper larger than your A4 mould and deckle by overlapping the edges of the sheets when couching them onto the blanket. By doing this your sheets can be as large as you like. However, your blankets, boards, and your press also need to be larger.

Extra large sheets

Extra large sheets of paper can be formed by using old flyscreen windows and door as a mould. The pulp can be poured onto the screen or sheets can be formed in a big vat. A child's paddling pool is good, or you can create your own vat in the size you need. Build a four-sided wooden frame with no top or bottom, and drape two sheets of heavy plastic over it. The plastic can be bought in hardware or paint shops as heavy plastic drop cloths. This forms a temporary large vat.

Form the sheets as usual, leave to dry them on the flyscreens, then peel them off and stack them. You can only make as many sheets of paper as you have flyscreens at one time. Begin early in the day, preferably when it is sunny, with a group of people to help. Prepare the pulp together, form the sheets on the flyscreens then leave them to dry. This takes time so perhaps you can talk to your friends and have lunch. Then peel the sheets of paper off the screens, stack them in a pile and form a second lot. At the end of the day the wooden frame can be dismantled and the plastic folded up until next time.

To make large sheets of paper, couch two A4 sheets side by side on the blanket, overlapping the edges.

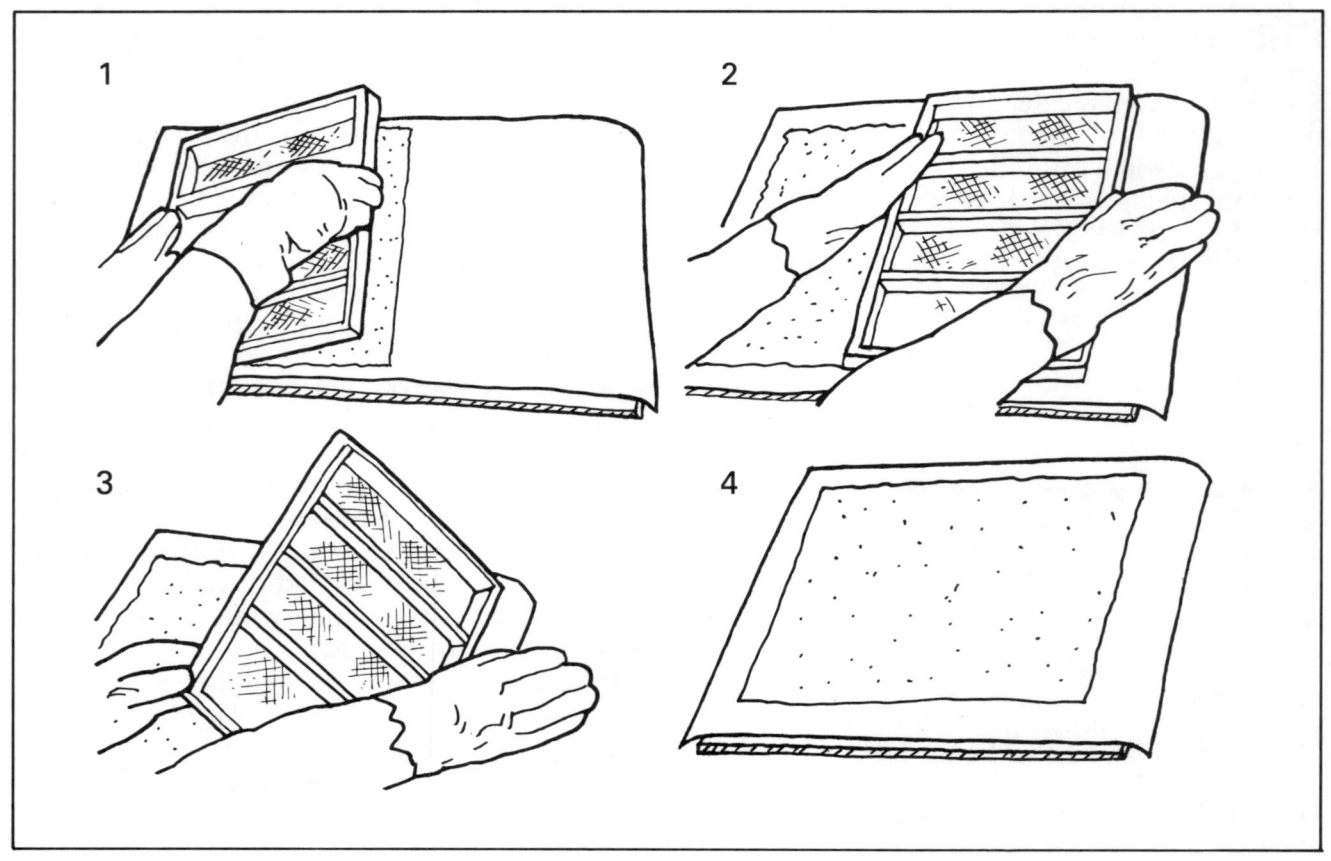

Colouring pulp

Recycled computer and copier paper tends to be a bit grey by itself because of the varied colours of inks on the papers in it. I find it best to recycle some coloured paper in each batch to add some life to it. Simply find a few sheets of paper of the same colour, rip them up, soak them and add them to your wet paper going through the blender. The longer you blend it the more even the colour will be. For more interesting variations, try the following ideas.

1 Try keeping a few shopping bags labelled with a colour. When you find a used red envelope from a Christmas card, pop it in the 'red' bag. When you receive a piece of junk mail on bright yellow paper, consign it to the 'yellow' bag. After a few weeks you will have collected papers in most colours you will want to use.

2 Buy some paper serviettes in a colour you like, use them for a dinner party, then recycle them. Rip up and soak the serviettes. Ignore any stains on them, they won't make a difference. Add shredded copy or computer paper to the mixture to make the colour go further and to add strength.

A shaped piece of paper can be created by masking off part of the screening of the mould with tape or contact paper. Form the sheet as usual.

Blend the papers and continue as described in 'Step by step from the beginning' on page 17. This paper will be very absorbent, just like the serviettes it started as, and will need to be sized. See page 32 for help with sizing.

3 Try using two vats of paper pulp: one white, one coloured. Dip one side of the mould and deckle in the coloured vat and couch it on your blankets. Dip your mould and deckle in the white vat and make a whole sheet. Couch this on top of your coloured pulp. The finished sheet will have one side all white, the other side partly white, partly coloured. Try dipping one corner or masking off a shape as described on page 34. Experiment yourself.

4 Watercolour, ink, tempera or gouache can be added to wet pulp for colour. Blend the pulp, drain off excess water and put it into a sealable plastic bag. Add the colourant to it and seal the bag. Pulp is much paler dry than wet, so keep this in mind when choosing how much colourant to add to pulp. Knead the colourant through the pulp until it is evenly distributed, then let it sit to soak in. Use the pulp as usual, being sure to wear gloves. The colourant will spread all through the water in the vat, but will be more concentrated in the pulp than if added directly to the vat. Remember, colourants will dye your vat, gloves, and your blankets, so wash everything when you are finished. Silver and gold gouache or ink added this way give a lovely iridescent sheen to the paper surface.

5 Colourant can also be added directly to your full vat of water and pulp; however, it will spread all through the water and become quite diluted. I prefer the method in point 4 above which concentrates the colourant in the pulp.

Try squirting coloured pulp onto a newly formed sheet of paper to create a pattern. (Painting with coloured pulps is described on page 38.)

6 If you are not concerned about permanence, then there are more choices. Food colouring, saffron, tea, turmeric or other natural dyes like boiled onion skins may be added to the pulp. These are perfect for children to work with. They fade over time, but add a bit of colour for today.

7 There are also dyes specifically designed for paper. These fuse with the fibres of the paper so that there is no colourant floating in the water. This makes them much more pleasant to work with. They are chemically stable and do not fade significantly over time. These dyes are not yet available in Australia, but can be ordered from Carriage House Paper in the United States (see Resources section).

> **HINT:** If you have two vats of differently coloured pulp, try this: form a plain sheet of paper in one colour and couch it on the blanket. Dry the mould and tape your shape on it. Make a shaped sheet of paper in the second colour and couch it on top of the first. This will give you your shape in one colour on a piece of paper of a second colour.

Embossing

Embossing is pressing something textured against a sheet of paper to create an impression on the paper. By embossing a sheet of paper as it is formed it is possible to capture the most intricate detail. Anything that is textured but reasonably flat can be used for embossing, so long as it is not damaged by water. See the photograph on page 42. Some of the things I have used are: lace, string, keys, satay sticks, decorative braids, crocheted doilies, plastic mesh orange bags, hessian, macrame, sushi mats, linoleum cut prints, woven place mats, gathered or heavily embroidered fabrics, bubble wrap, and lace collars. Fabric with a woven or raised embroidered design can be used in place of plain blankets. Many things can be used to emboss — I am always discovering something new to try. What can you think of?

Remember that if you have added inks or paints to your pulp it will stain anything pressed into

String can be laid on a newly formed sheet of paper to emboss a linear design.

it. Do not use anything precious. Alternatively, try embossing white (undyed) paper and painting it later.

How to emboss paper

1 Begin by making a new post of paper.

2 Couch a thick sheet of paper onto your blankets, or two sheets on top of each other if your pulp is becoming thin.

3 Lay your textured piece flat on the surface of the newly formed sheet of paper and press gently. Leave it there and cover with another blanket. A thin cotton or synthetic blanket is not enough here. Add a couple of thick wool blankets, wadding, or layer of foam. This gives the textured piece a soft surface to press into and prevents the texture embossing through to the next sheet.

4 Continue making more sheets on your post of paper.

5 Put the paper into the press for an hour or so, then take it out and leave it to dry on a flat surface *with the textured piece still in place*. Only remove the textured piece when the paper is completely dry. This ensures you get the most detailed impression.

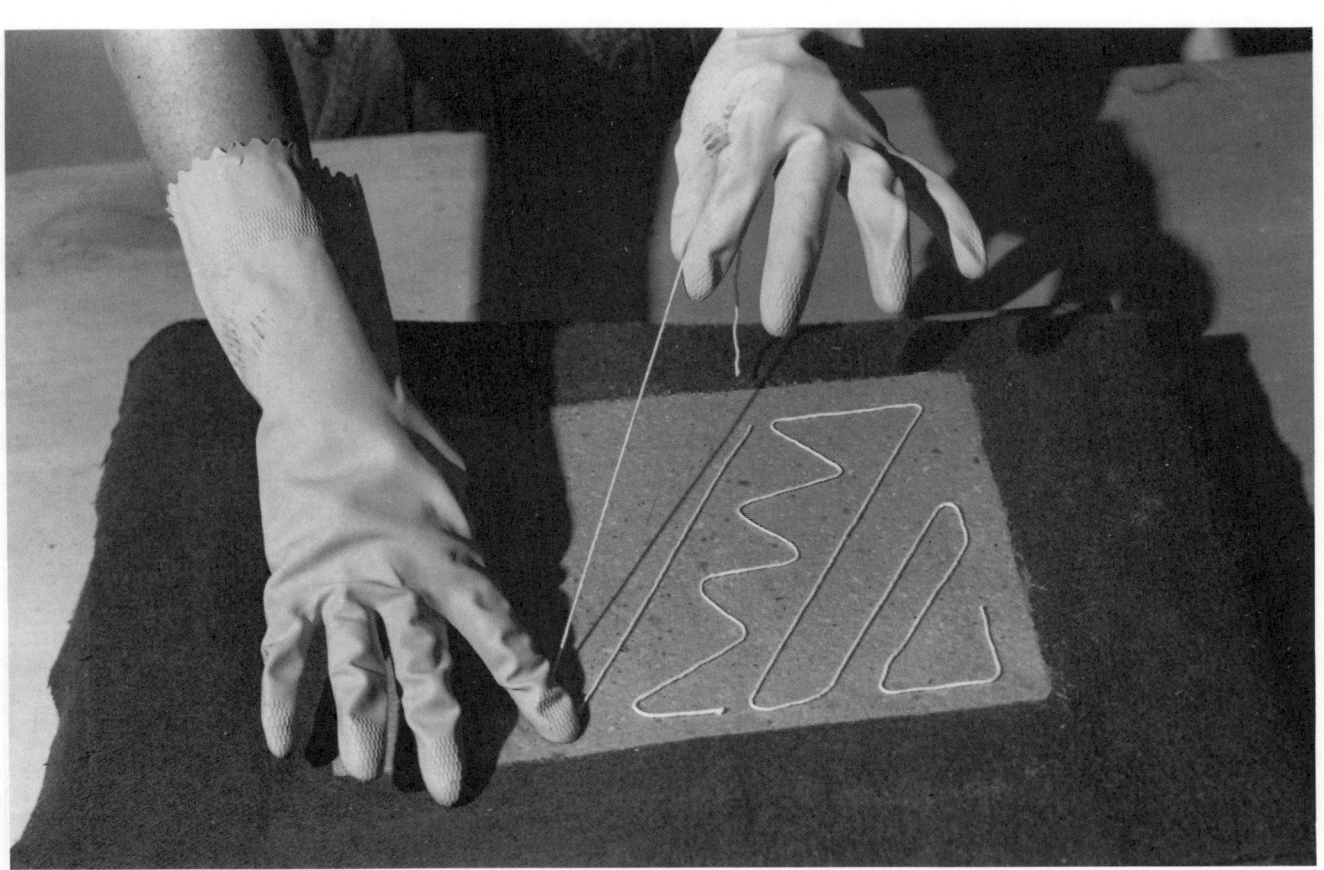

Decorating embossed papers

Pastels or paint lightly applied (dry brush technique) to the raised surface of the paper highlights the texture of embossed papers. See 'Embossed papers' in the centre colour spread for examples. Car retouch paints in spray cans from hardware stores or airbrushing also help highlight texture. Spray across the papers from an oblique angle. Be sure to work in a well-ventilated area.

Watermarks

A watermark traditionally identifies the name or logo of the papermaker and is common on quality stationery. A watermark is easy to see when the paper is held up to the light.

You can create your own watermark by shaping a length of wire into an image or your initials. Reverse any type so that it will end up reading correctly. Cut it to size with wire cutters and file off the sharp edges. Hammer it flat. Then sew or solder the wire onto the screen of

A watermark will give your paper a thoroughly professional touch.

the mould and make paper as usual. If sewing, use synthetic thread — polyester or nylon — which will not rot in water. The wire presses into the sheet, creating your image in an area of thinner, more translucent, paper.

Painting with coloured pulps

Start by making pulp from different coloured papers, keeping each colour separate. Do not add any extra water to the pulps after blending. Fill plastic sauce bottles with the coloured pulps. These can be used to draw with by squirting coloured pulp over a wet sheet of paper just couched on a blanket, as shown in the photograph on page 36. Also see the A4 stationery paper in the photograph opposite page 17 for an example of this process. Pulps can also be used to make a sheet of paper, in any shape or design, by squeezing pulp directly onto a blanket and pressing that. Have a go!

Images can also be built by working with the pulp as if it were clay. Strain the excess water out of the pulp and form flat shapes on the wet blanket. Build up a sheet of paper with these adjoining shapes in various colours. Make sure

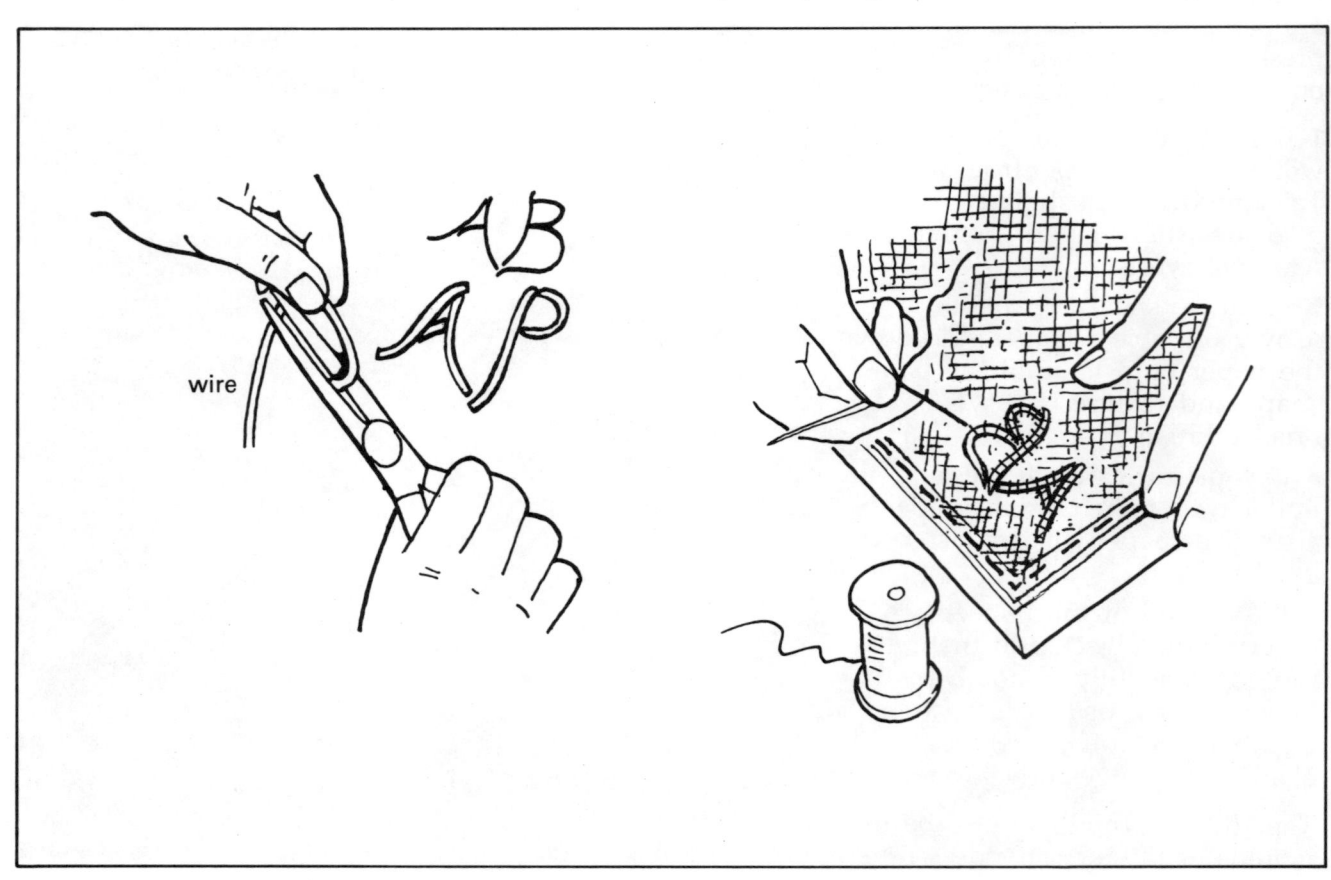

the shapes butt against each other so that they fuse together in the pressing. When your pulp painting is complete, smooth a blanket over it and press as usual. Sizing can be added to give the paper strength if the piece is large.

Casting paper

Casting is a process by which you can shape paper into three-dimensional forms. You can use pressed sheets of paper or newly blended pulp. Your choice depends on which you are most comfortable working with, and the nature of what you are casting. Deep irregular shapes will work better with pulp. Flatter surface designs, angular or softly curving shapes will work well with sheets. A very large piece may need a frame of wire or fabric mesh to help support it.

Scraps of acid-free mount board, free for the asking from a framer, will work well for pulp. They already have some glue in the paper, which adds strength. Cotton linters are also good but will need sizing. Sizing gives increased strength, particularly important if the piece is large.

Sheet method
The simplest form of casting is to drape a *thick* pressed sheet of paper over a textured object, a bowl or the side of a basket.

1 Begin by coating the object in something that will prevent the paper from sticking to the form. Talcum powder, a spray cooking oil, a thin coat of dishwashing liquid, or thin strips of plastic wrap will work.

2 Pick up a sheet of paper on its blanket, drape it over the object, paper side down, and press the paper onto it, until the paper takes on its shape and texture. Use your fingers or a stiff bristled brush to do this.

3 If you can, carefully peel off the blanket. If not, leave it there until the paper is drier and try again. The paper will dry faster without the wet blanket.

4 If a second or third sheet is needed to finish covering the object, add that now, overlapping the edges slightly. Smooth the join with your fingers or a bristle brush to meld the edges together. Blot off the excess water with a dry blanket or sponge and leave to dry slowly.

The sheet method can also be used with large moulds of plaster, carved styrofoam sheets, or sewn fabric shapes filled with sand. With the sewn shape, leave one end open to drain out the sand when the paper has dried. Carefully pull out the fabric shape and your three-dimensional paper sculpture is left.

In each case, cover the mould sheet by sheet, overlapping the edges as you go, until the whole mould is covered. Press each sheet meticulously into all your carved detail. Blot off excess water and leave to dry as before. If the piece is large it may need more than one thickness of paper to support itself. Paint methyl cellulose between the layers to help bond them together. Sizing can also be used to add strength to the structure.

Pulp method
The pulp method uses blended pulp that has had the excess water strained out of it, as shown on page 23. The pulp is worked a bit like clay. Take a handful of pulp and press it evenly into your mould. Keep going until the whole mould is evenly covered with pulp. Do not design a mould with any undercutting or your paper will not come out! Again, blot off the excess water, and leave to dry. When the paper is completely dry it will peel away from the mould quite easily, starting at one edge.

Making your own moulds

If you can't find an object you want to cast, you can create your own moulds in either styrofoam or plaster, as shown in the photograph on page 40.

Making a styrofoam mould
Styrofoam is light and easy to handle. First find some styrofoam from packing for electrical goods or fruit boxes. Making a mould out of styrofoam can be done in one of two ways. You can cut into the sheet with a craft knife, using a sharp new blade. Remember to change the blade frequently so that your cuts are clean and do not rip through the styrofoam.

The second method is to use a soldering iron. The heat from the soldering iron will melt the styrofoam so it can be used to carve out the shape you want to cast. This process creates toxic fumes, so work in a well-ventilated area, preferably outside. Between uses, rest the soldering iron on its stand on top of a hotplate to prevent it burning your working surface. Never leave it unattended, particularly if children are around. A soldering iron in curious hands could cause a bad burn or start a fire.

How to make a plaster mould

Plaster of Paris, which is good for small moulds, or pottery plaster, which is stronger, can be used to make moulds for casting paper. Pottery plaster is available from pottery supply shops. It has the added advantage of being usable over and over again without the plaster crumbling. Plaster-coated bandages may also be suitable for some projects.

The object you wish to cast should not be able to absorb water or the plaster will stick to it. Seal it with a polyurethane varnish such as Estapol or a layer of wax. Then coat the object with some sort of release agent, such as a thin coat of spray cooking oil, talcum powder, dishwashing liquid or vaseline.

Plasticene can also be used to sculpt objects for casting and can be peeled out of the plaster later. It may also be used to form ridges around objects that need to be cast in more than one section. Look at the object carefully. Can you visualise the section of plaster pulling straight off the object? Or are there undercuts that will prevent this? Avoid right angles; they are tricky to remove from the plaster. Use rounded corners or a tapered shape instead of one with straight sides. Alternatively, the plaster itself can be made into a block and carved.

When mixing plaster always add the plaster to the water, not the other way around. Start by calculating the volume of your mould which determines how much water you need. Next you need to know how much plaster to mix with it. The plaster may come with a recipe on it, but if not, the ratio of plaster to water is 1.38 parts plaster to 1 part water by weight. It is important to be precise. Use cold water to produce the smoothest surface in the plaster. If you use hot water or stir the mixture as you add the plaster the setting time will be shorter and you will produce a grainier surface to the mould. Large moulds may need a layer of flyscreen or some kind of reinforcement in the plaster.

Moulds for casting paper can be formed out of plaster (*left*) or styrofoam (*right*) using a small craft knife. Styrofoam can also be shaped with a hot soldering iron, but be sure to work in a well-ventilated place or outdoors, because the fumes are toxic.

Thick-pressed sheets of paper can be manipulated into three-dimensional sculptural forms. Try crumpling, folding and twisting the paper. Be gentle and take your time. When you are happy with what you have made, leave it to dry.

Manipulating paper

Manipulating paper is working with paper as a three-dimensional sculptural medium. Start by forming a few sheets of thick paper. When you lift the newly-formed sheets off the deckle, they should be 5–7 millimetres thick on the surface of the mould. After doing this once, you will see what thickness of paper *you* want for your project.

Press the paper a little longer than usual so that it is dry enough to handle. Peel apart the sheets as usual, but instead of laying them to dry on a flat surface, peel off the blanket as well and manipulate the paper by itself. Try crumpling, folding, twisting and curling the paper, as shown in the photograph above, but be gentle with it or it will tear. Take your time. The paper is still quite fragile, but after a few mistakes you will get a sense of what it can take. The paper can be manipulated by itself or draped over an object.

When you like what you have done leave it to dry.

To create larger pieces glue sheets of paper together and press overlapping edges together. Methyl cellulose (wallpaper paste) or PVA can be used as glue. Both are also good for painting on the finished piece when dry to help it hold its shape and add strength. Gesso can also be painted on the back of small pieces for support.

41

Projects with handmade paper

By now you have mastered basic sheet forming and experimented with a few of the techniques in the last few pages. You have created a collection of papers that are uniquely your own. Most likely, some of them turned out differently from what you intended. I find I often learn the most from mistakes and happy accidents, so do not be afraid to experiment. Like any new skill, paper-making becomes easier with practice.

The next question is 'what do I do with my paper?' Handmade paper can be used in combination with many other crafts: calligraphy, book-binding, collage, decoupage, to cover boxes, basket weaving, three-dimensional artwork, print-making, stationery, or for machine embroidery. The list is long. For beginners, it may be hard to know just where to start. To make it easier, I have described several projects here for you to try. Have a go at them, then see what other ideas come to mind. These projects are only to get you started. Paper can be used for so many things — the only limit is your imagination.

Wallet folder

See the peach coloured wallet folder with ribbons in the colour photo facing page 33. Wallet folders are useful for carrying small items: cosmetics, receipts, credit cards, paper clips, buttons. The outside piece can be made with embossed paper or decorated with machine embroidery, painting or calligraphy, or left plain as in the photo.

Equipment needed
Two A4 sheets of fairly heavy handmade paper, one having a deckle edge; a pencil, needle and thread; a bone folder (see glossary) or the edge of a spoon; ruler, PVA glue, inexpensive bristle brush, narrow ribbon and one button in colours that harmonise with your paper; a cutting mat or sheet of cardboard, and a craft knife with a new blade in it.

These work well for embossing textures into paper: string, corrugated cardboard, keys, lace, the side of a basket, a crocheted belt, braids, straw floor mats, sushi mats or cane blinds, satay sticks, crocheted placemats, lino cuts, plastic mesh and loosely woven fabric. See page 37.

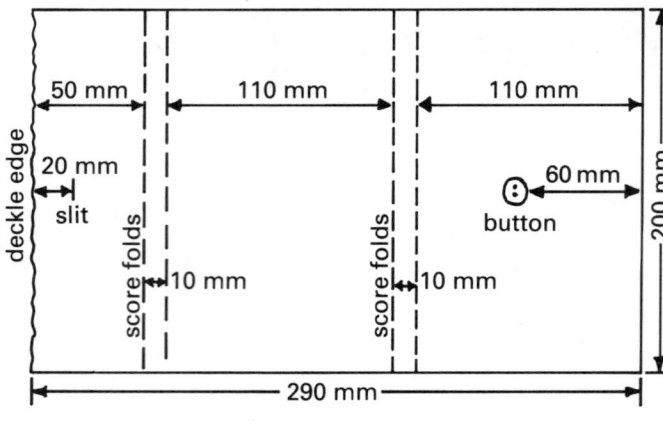

50 mm | 110 mm | 110 mm

deckle edge

20 mm
slit

score folds ↔10 mm

score folds ↔10 mm

60 mm
button

200 mm

← 290 mm →

— — — line for scoring folds

1 Get out your sheet of paper with the deckle edge. With the ruler and craft knife, trim the two long sides and one short side to 200 mm × 290 mm, as shown below.

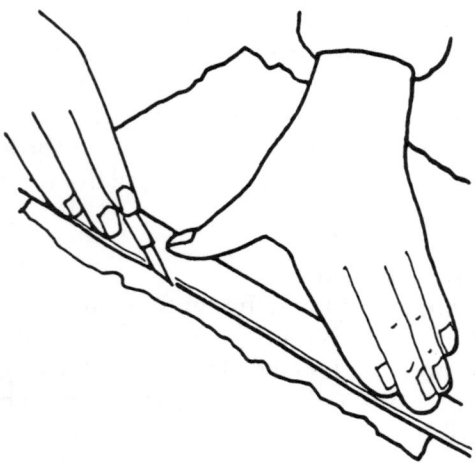

2 Lightly mark the placement of folds along one edge.

3 Using the triangle as an edge, score each fold across the paper with the bone folder.

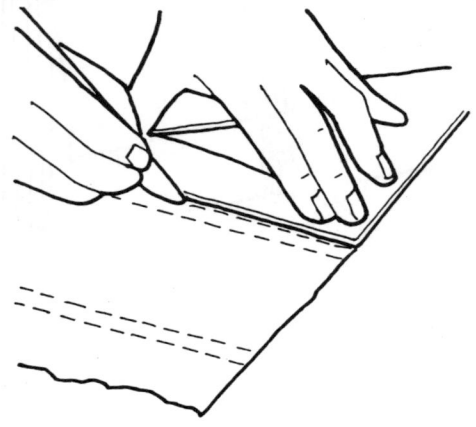

4 Measure the middle of the folder along the end with the deckle edge and cut the slit for the ribbons, 20 mm in from the edge.

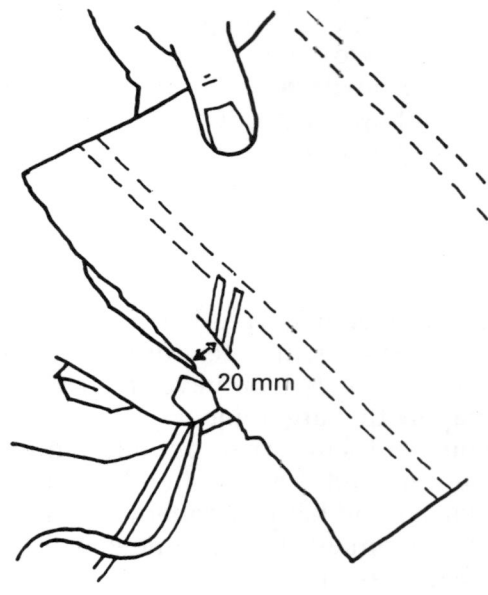

20 mm

5 Feed the ribbons through the slit from the outside of the folder to the inside. Glue 10 mm of the ends on the inside. Leave to dry.

6 Cut a small square of the leftover paper to cover the ends of the ribbon. Brush glue on it and let it get tacky. Place the square over ribbon ends.

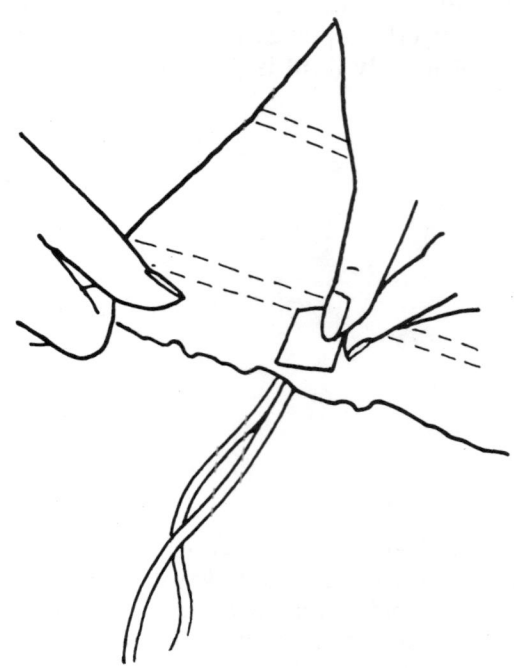

7 On the inside of the folder measure the centre on the opposite end, 60 mm in from the edge, for the button placement. Glue a 3-mm wide strip of paper over this centre point. This will prevent your sewing ripping through the paper. Leave to dry. Pierce two holes in the paper on either side of the strip with the needle. Sew the button on the outside of the folder, the stitches going through the reinforcing strip. Knot the beginning and ending of the thread together.

8 Cut a small square of paper from your leftover scraps to cover the sewing. Brush glue on the square and let it get tacky. Press the square in position over the sewing.

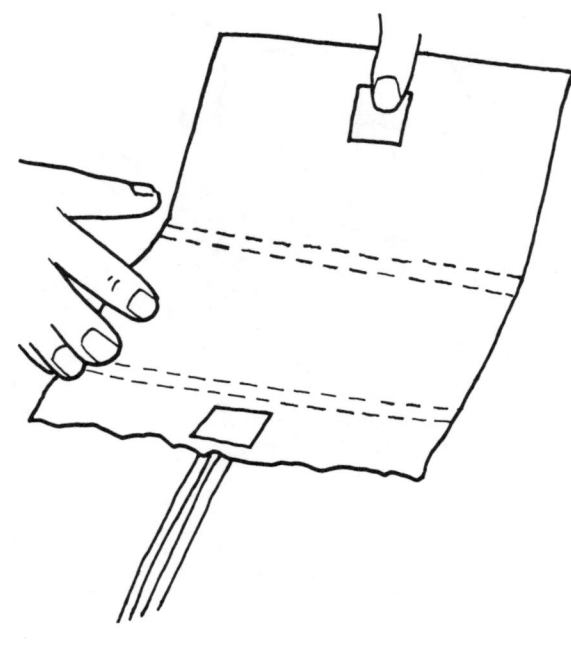

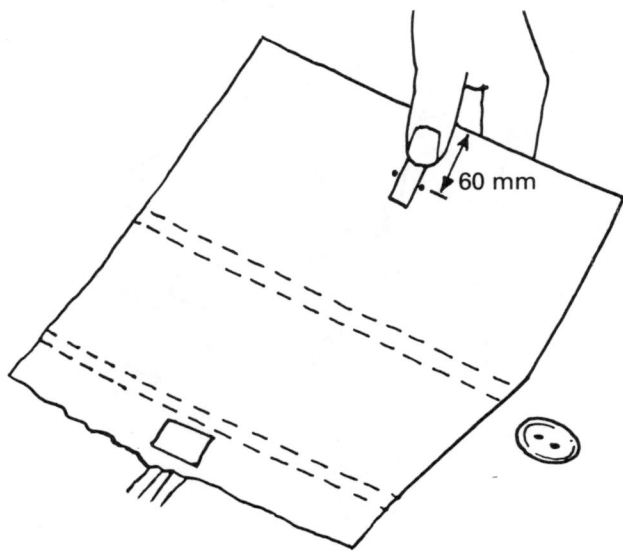

9 Cut two strips (9.5 cm × 12.5 cm) for the sides of the folder from the second sheet of A4 paper. Round the corners.

10 Leave 10-mm tabs on each end and accordion-fold the strips in between. Make the folds equal.

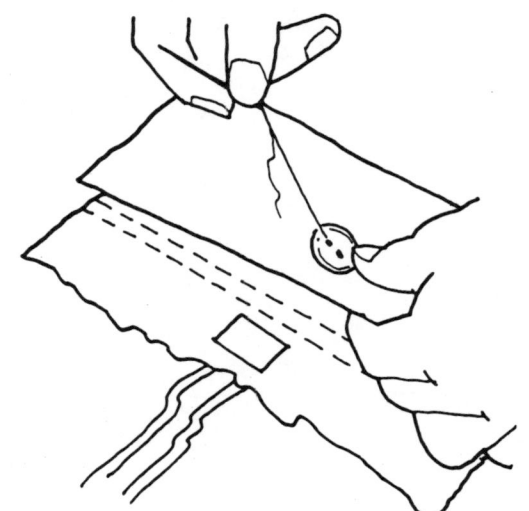

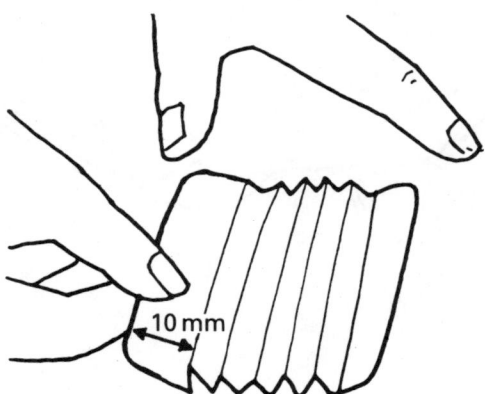

11 Glue tabs on the accordion-folded sides. Leave to get tacky. Place one tab in position and press firmly, then do the second. Repeat on second side.

12 The folder is finished. To close it, fold the deckle-edged flap down towards the button. Wrap the ribbons around the whole folder, then wind the ribbons around the button. This will hold the folder closed. If the folder is to be handled a lot, protect the surface of the paper with a spray of fixative, mat varnish or a thin coat of PVA glue.

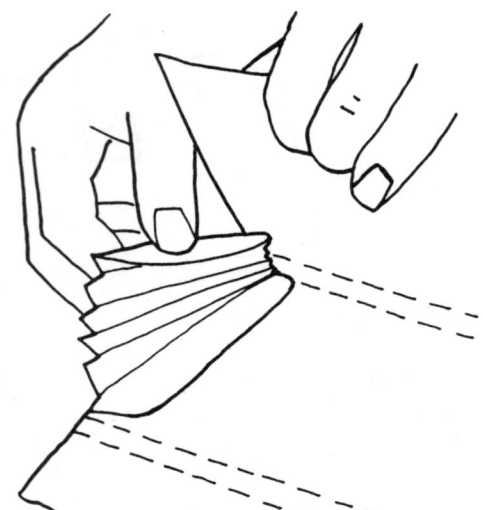

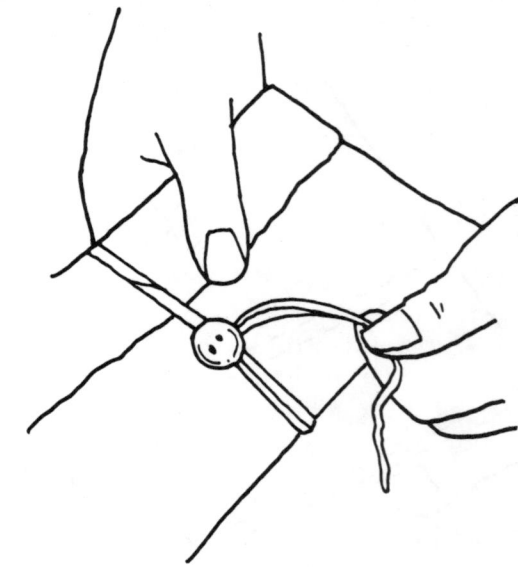

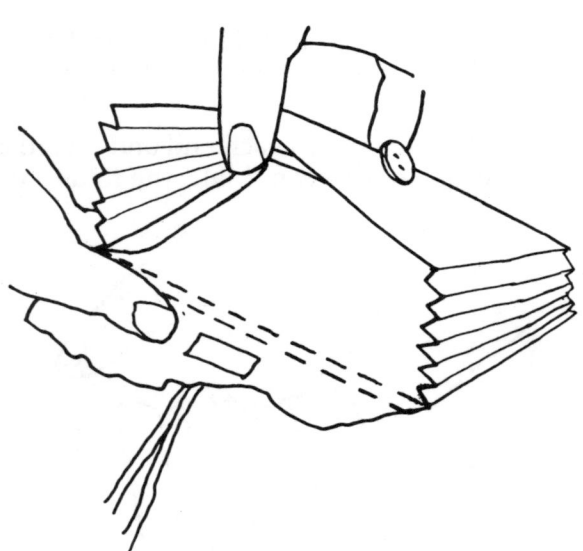

Presentation folder

A folder decorated with your own handmade embossed paper is a useful and unusual gift for just about anyone. Even people who 'have everything' rarely have anything like this. See photo facing page 48 for an example of these folders. They have a pocket inside to hold papers or photos and are perfect for distinctive business presentations.

Equipment needed

Two pieces of A4 embossed paper (or one A3), painted or decorated as you like, and a sheet of heavy, stiff commercial paper such as Stonehenge (245 g) for the folder itself; a craft knife, cutting mat or large sheet of cardboard; pencil, ruler, triangle (or set square); old newspapers, PVA glue, inexpensive bristle brush; a bone folder or substitute.

Be sure you have clean hands and a clean workspace before beginning so the paper does not become marked. See the section on embossing for ideas.

1 Mark out the folder on the paper lightly in pencil as shown in the diagram below.

2 Score all the folds, with the bone folder or the edge of a spoon. This allows you to fold paper precisely on a clean straight line.

3 Put your cutting mat or sheet of cardboard out on your work surface. Cut out the folder along your drawn lines, always using a ruler to cut against.

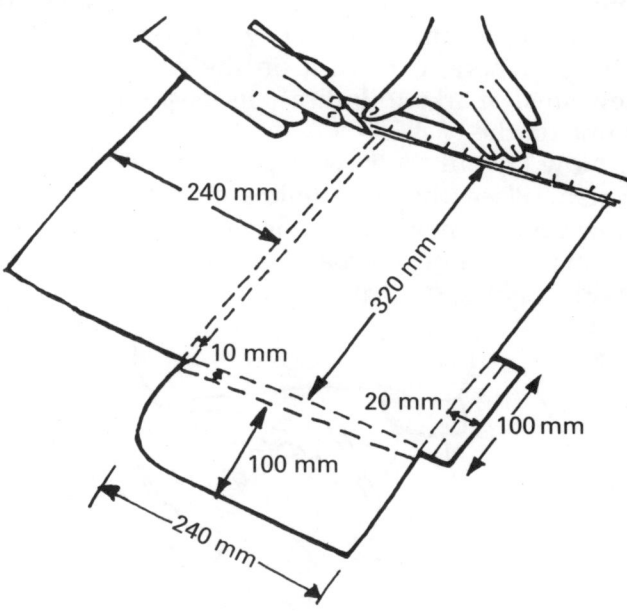

4 Place a ruler on one of the scored lines, holding it with one hand. Place the other hand on the other side of the paper and bend it up at the scored fold. Run a finger along it to make sure it is well creased. If it is not easy to fold, re-score it. Continue until all the scored lines are folded.

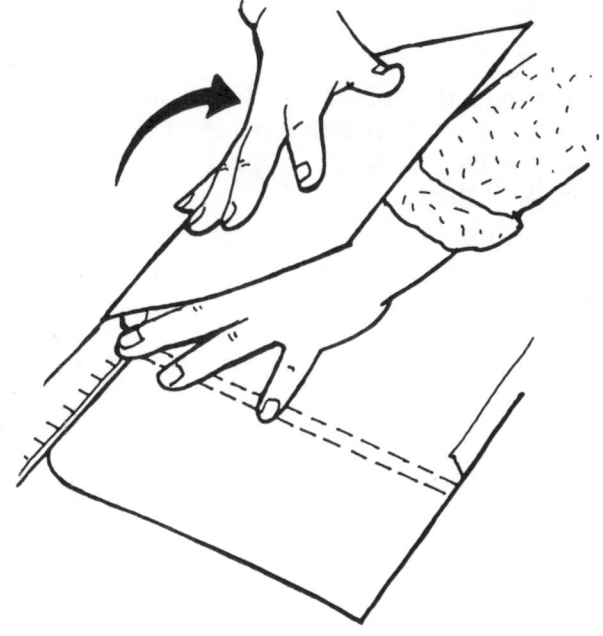

47

5 Place your embossed paper on the front cover of the folder and have a look at it. Are you happy with it? You can decorate both covers or just the front. You may want to decorate your embossed paper with inks, paints, pastels, calligraphy or machine embroidery. You may want to leave it plain. My folders are painted with metallic inks and highlighted with pastels to show off the embossing. Do what you like. Then choose where to place it on the cover. Make a few small marks to indicate its position. Do the same on the back.

Now lay out the newspaper and the glue and brush. Place the two embossed artworks face down on the newspaper. Brush the PVA glue in an even coat on the back of the embossed artworks, taking particular care with the edges.

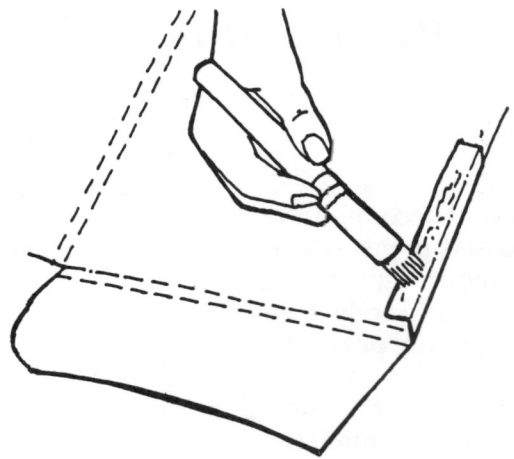

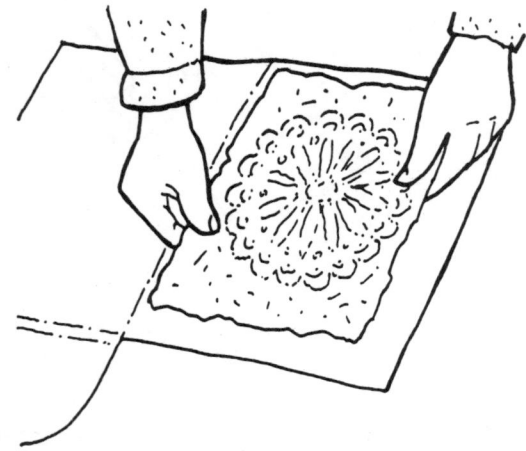

6 Leave them to dry until the glue begins to turn clear and is very tacky. Place one on the front cover of your folder to your marks and press it down firmly.

7 Turn over the folder and lay it on your work surface. Carefully rub the inside of the folder to be sure it is well stuck. Repeat the process for the back of the folder.

8 Brush glue on the tab on the folder's pocket, and leave it to get tacky. Bend in position and press the tab to adhere.

9 Find a thin book or a stack of papers to fill the pocket to the thickness of the spine. This will help it hold its shape. Check there are no drips of glue on the front or back. Place the folder on a clean surface and stack a couple of large, heavy books on top of it. Telephone books work well. Leave the folder to dry for a few hours and it is done!

10 There are many options for decorating the cover of a folder. You can cut strips of various papers you have made, weave them together, then glue them on to the covers as above, or make a collage of papers.

These three folders decorated with embossed papers make great gift ideas. Even people who have everything don't have one of these.

Placemats

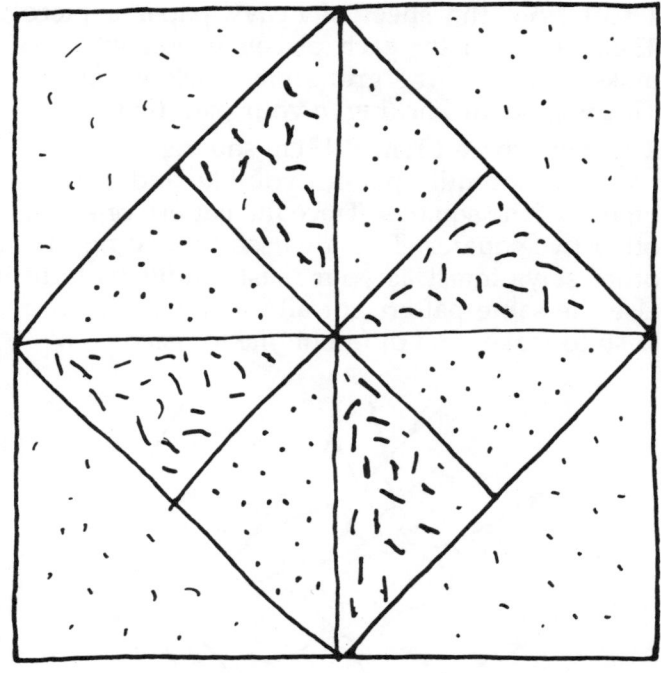

Colourful placemats made from handmade paper are a distinctive item to grace your table. Using your own papers makes them unique, and laminating them in plastic makes them durable enough to stand up to day-to-day wear. See the photo opposite as an example. Any quilt pattern can be used — two of the many possibilities are shown here. The colours of the paper can be chosen to match your decor.

Equipment needed
Six or seven A4 sheets of handmade paper in coordinated colours for each placemat, gluestick or PVA glue and an inexpensive bristle brush (for glue), sewing machine, coordinated thread, one sheet of heavy drawing or coloured paper, one sheet of tracing paper, craft knife and extra blades, cutting mat or sheet of cardboard, triangle or set square, ruler, quilt pattern, drawing paper.

Choose a mix of some light papers and some quite dark. This makes the patterns more eye-catching.

Placemats — quilt patterns

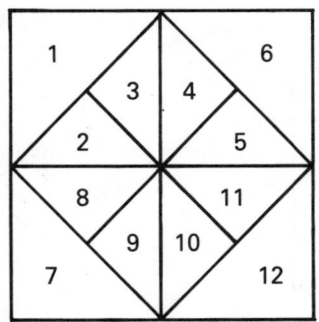 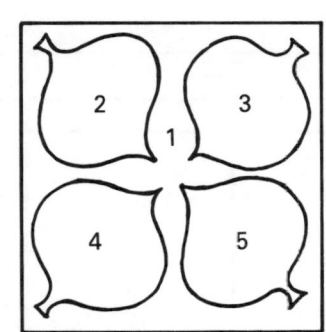

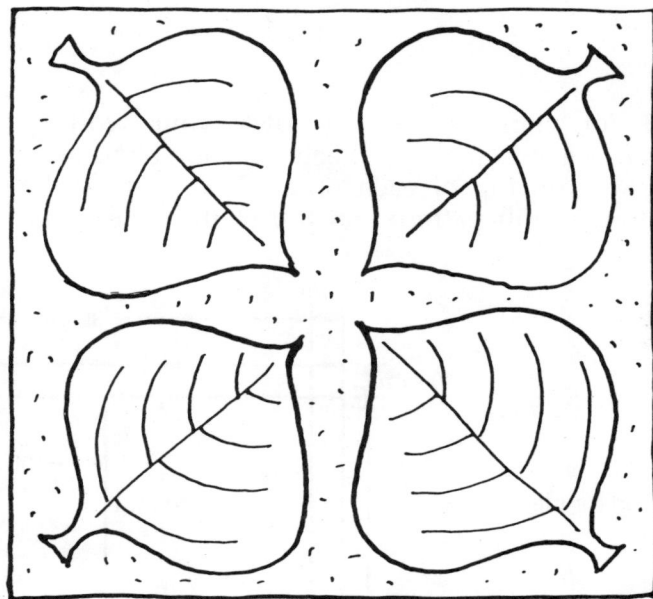

Sewn quilt pattern placemats are an unusual and durable item to grace your table. Any quilt pattern can be used and you can choose the colour to match your decor.

1 Cut from the sheet of heavy paper a piece 43 cm × 30 cm for each placemat you want to make. Rule out the grid shown below onto it. This will be the backing to your placemat.

2 Cut out three 13 cm × 13 cm squares of tracing paper. Pick a quilt pattern you like and draw it on one of the squares. Trace the pattern onto the other two squares. Two are used for cutting, the other stays intact as your master quilt pattern. Use the same pattern for all the placemats you wish to make, or a different one for each.

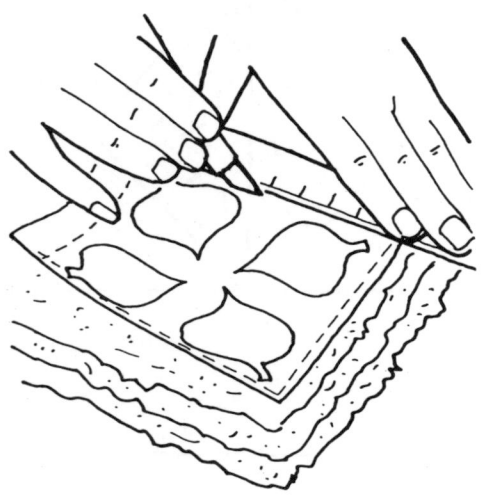

3 Put your cutting mat over your working surface. Stack three sheets of your handmade paper on top of each other. Place one of the drawn quilt patterns on top of them near one

corner. With the craft knife and the ruler, cut through the three sheets of paper along the lines of your pattern. With the pattern shown in the example, cut out the squares first, then the leaves separately.

4 Take another of the quilt pattern squares and place it on top of the remaining half of your stack of three sheets of paper. Cut the shapes out. Change the blade in your knife if needed.

5 Check the measurements on the grid and cut out the border strips and corners. I used the irregular deckle edge on the outside. You will need to piece two strips together for the borders on the long sides. Now you have all the pieces cut out for the first placemat.

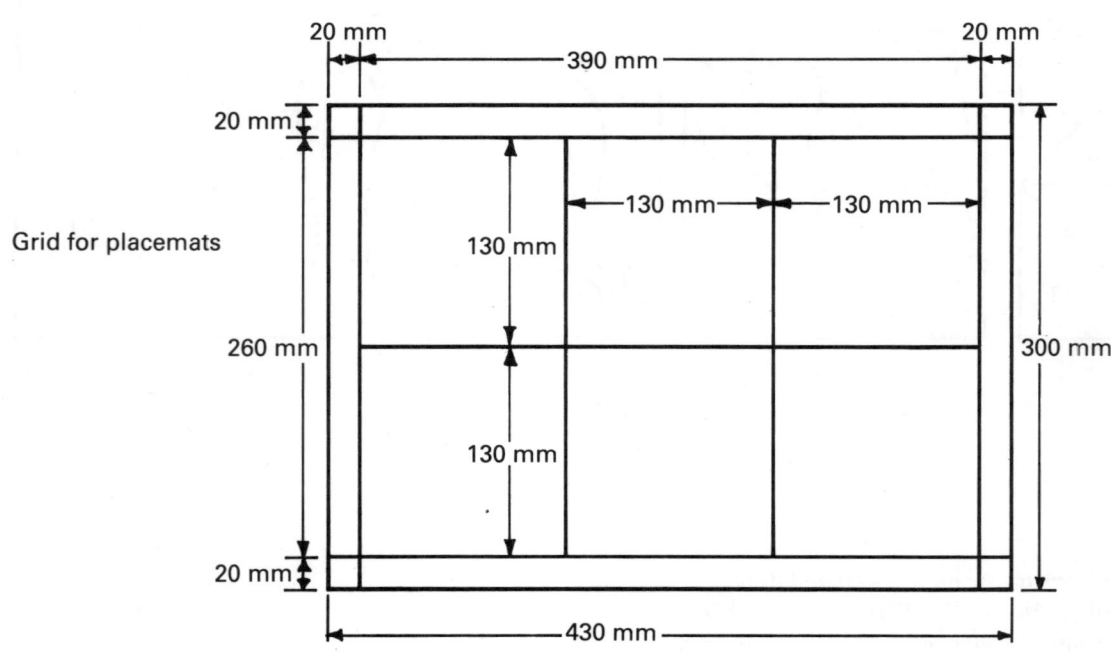

Grid for placemats

6 Distribute the cut paper shapes across the squares in the grid, mixing the colours as you go. With the pattern shown, the squares are laid down first and the leaves positioned on top.

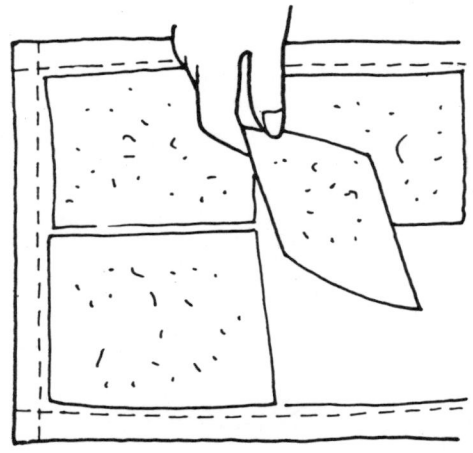

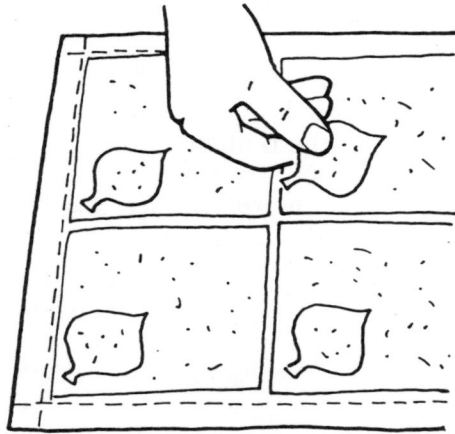

Then the borders are put in place. Look the whole placemat over and mix and match the colours until you are happy with the balance. This may take a little fiddling.

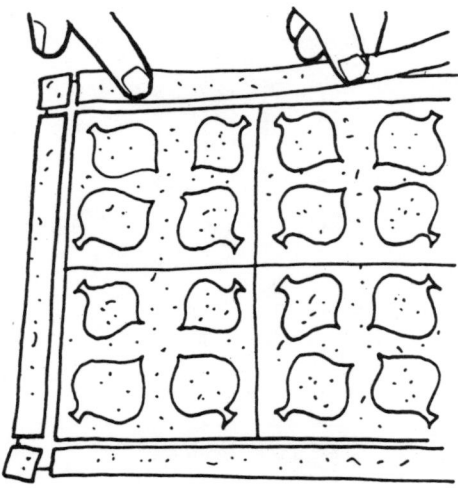

7 Put a dab of glue on the back of each shape. Do not use a lot of glue or the shapes will be harder to sew. Glue down all the shapes and the borders, matching them to the squares drawn on the heavy paper grid.

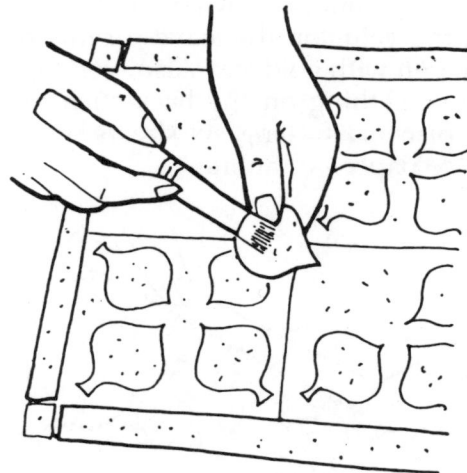

8 Stack some books on the placemat and leave it to dry completely, overnight if possible. The glue must be completely dry before sewing.

9 Start the next placemat and follow the same steps to make as many placemats as you want.

10 Choose a contrasting colour for your thread. Set it up as your top thread on the sewing machine.

11 Set the sewing machine for a satin or zig zag stitch at the widest setting and 8 to 10 stitches per centimetre (20 stitches per inch). Do not make the stitches any closer together or the needle will rip a line through the paper. Try a practice piece.

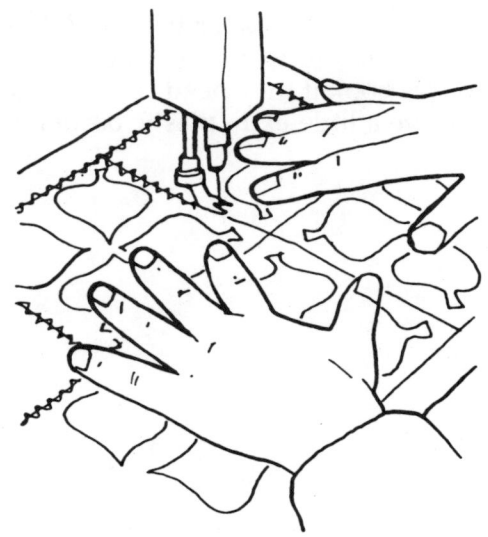

12 Sew all the edges of the papers, covering up the gaps in between them. Have someone else look at it to see if you missed any spots. I did! This will take time; it is exacting work. Repeat for each placemat. Cut all the threads.

13 Sign your name somewhere on the front and draw in the veins on the leaves of this pattern. I chose a pen with gold ink. Also, you may want to write something on the back such as: 'June 1993 — placemats using six sheets of my own handmade paper — Pauline.'

14 Look up 'laminating' in the yellow pages in your area. You should be able to laminate a placemat for under $10. The laminators may not have seen handmade paper before and may be concerned about it working. Show them the photo in this book if they need reassurance. Ask them to leave a little extra plastic border around the edge.

Handbound books

What more appropriate use for handmade paper than a handbound book? You can use commercial paper for the inside pages, though for a very special book, your finest handmade paper would be ideal. Make it small — an autograph book — or large — a sketch book of sized art-quality paper. See the handbound books in the photo facing page 33 for an example.

Equipment needed
Two heavy sheets of handmade paper for the cover; a cutting mat, craft knife and extra blades; a metal ruler and triangle or set square; papers for inside, either handmade or commercial; heavy linen or embroidery thread in a coordinated colour, a bulldog clip or clothes peg, a large needle, an electric drill, a 1.5 mm to 3 mm drill bit (depending on how big the book is and what you have available), a nail, a hammer and scrap newspaper.

1 Get out the papers, cutting mat, triangle, knife, and blades. Put a new sharp blade in your knife. Choose what size you want your book (up to A4) and how many pages it will have. It can be horizontal or vertical. My books have 20 to 25 pages.

2 Line up the papers in an even stack before cutting. Mark the size of the book on the top sheet of paper in pencil, using the triangle and ruler to ensure accuracy.

3 Cut the papers to whatever size you want the book to be, using the metal ruler for an edge. It takes several passes to cut a stack of papers with a knife. Do not try to cut them in one go. Use medium pressure and keep the knife tilted.

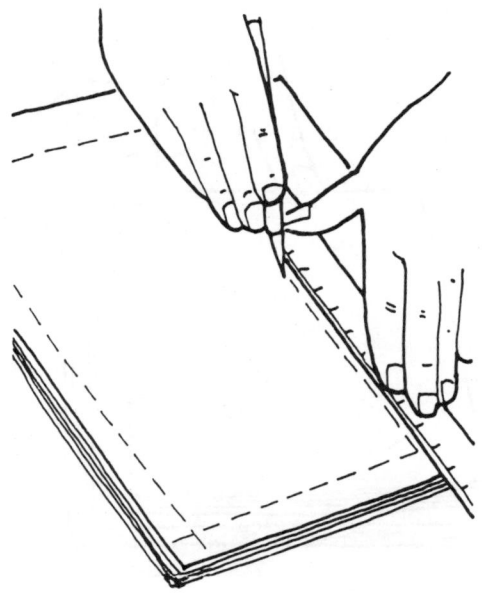

4 All the holes will be 10 mm in from the spine. Mark holes every 20 mm to 30 mm along this line, starting 10 mm in from each end.

5 Use a bulldog clip to hold the papers together. Lightly hammer a nail into the holes where marked, holding the stack of papers on a scrap block of wood. Give the nail just one good tap. This is not to puncture the papers, just to make an indentation so the drill won't slip.

6 Fit a drill bit in the drill. Place the drill in the first indentation and switch it on. Drill holes through the stack of papers. Take care. If you are not comfortable using the drill, ask someone for help.

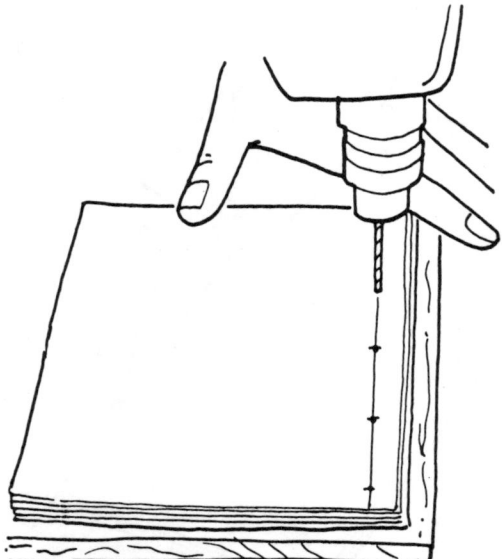

7 Get out the papers you have chosen for the covers. Place one of the inside pages on top of the covers. Cut the two covers 1 mm larger in both dimensions than the inside pages.

8 Place the two covers on the bottom of the stack of papers. Poke a needle through the holes in the stack to pierce the covers, thus matching the holes in the inside papers. This is cleaner than drilling the covers. Position the covers at the front and back of the book.

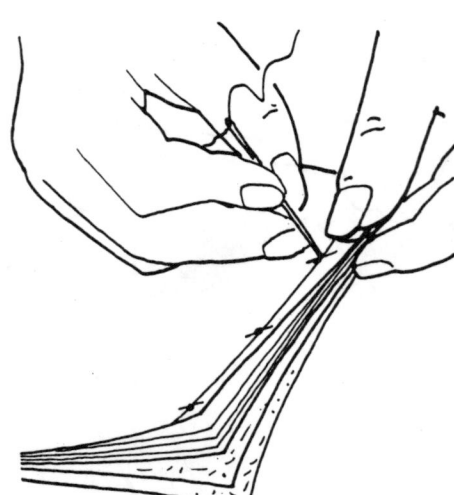

9 Measure out thread to four times the book's length.

10 The sewing looks terribly complicated but it isn't. Start at one end of the binding, leaving the thread end to tie later.

11 Sew up to the next hole, then once around the book's spine. Again, sew up to the next hole, then once around the book's spine. Keep going to the far end.

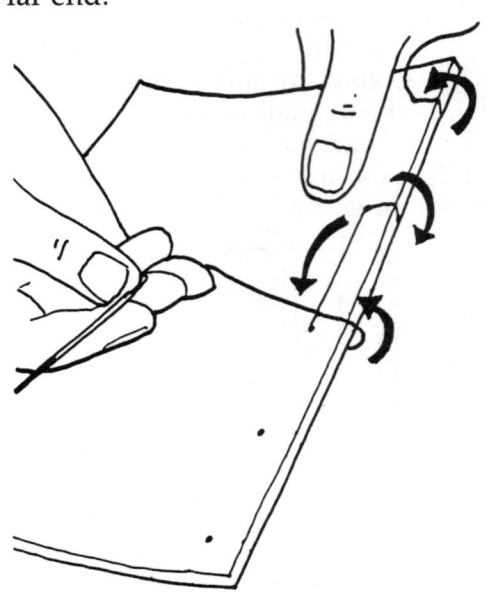

12 At the end do one stitch around the top edge of the book and begin sewing back. This time just sew from hole to hole, not around the spine. Your stitches will fill the gaps. This will bring you back to where you started. Tie the ends, and you have a finished handmade book.

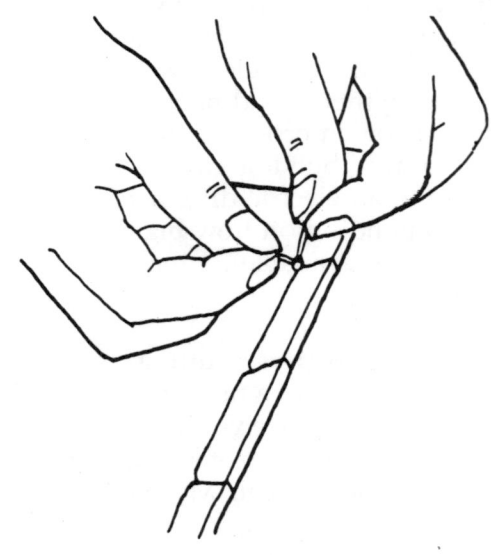

Striped brooches and earrings

Paper jewellery? Why not? You can create your own stunning designs using your own paper, and, following the method below, your jewellery will be light and durable. See the pieces in the colour photograph facing page 33.

Equipment needed

A selection of handmade papers of the same thickness in various colours; a pencil, cardboard (white if available), PVA glue; an inexpensive bristle brush for glue; a craft knife and extra blades; a triangle, cutting mat (or sheet of cardboard); metal ruler; a few scraps of narrow, brightly coloured ribbon; old newspapers; and brooch backs and earring clips.

1 Set up the cutting mat, craft knife and papers. Cut narrow strips of varying widths, 2 mm to 5 mm wide, in each of your colours. Have some papers that are light and some dark so the stripes show up well.

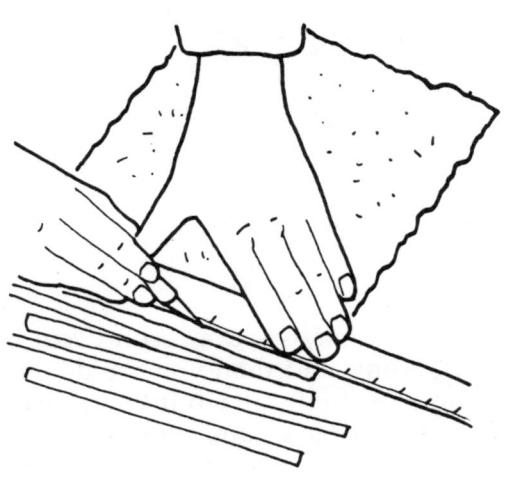

2 Pick out the ribbons in colours that harmonise with the papers. Paint a thin layer of glue on one side of the ribbons. Leave to dry. When dry, this will stiffen the ribbon, making it easier to handle and easier to cut without fraying.

3 Get out the cardboard. Think about what you want to make. A brooch? Earrings? What shape? Oval, round, square or rectangular? Look at the pieces in the colour photograph for ideas but do not be limited by them. Draw the shapes you want onto the cardboard in pencil. Make sure the corners are square. The sizes I used were 65 mm × 25 mm for the brooches and 25 mm × 25 mm for earrings. Choose what is right for you; some people like larger jewellery than others. Cut out a few shapes to start.

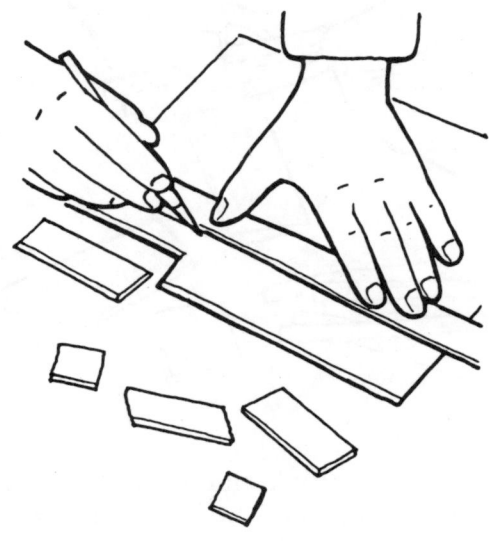

4 Brush PVA glue onto one side of the first shape. Cover right out to all the edges. Leave to get tacky.

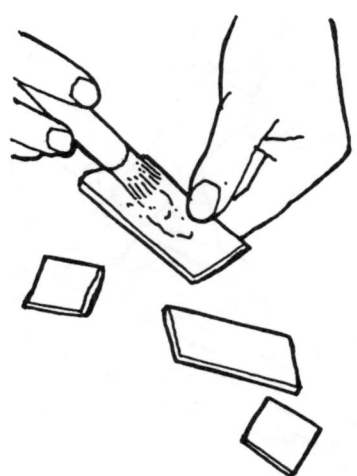

5 Look at your coloured strips of paper. The darker ones work best on the ends, with a mix of colours and widths in between. Choose what you want to try on the first piece.

6 Starting at one end of the cardboard, and flush with its edge, place a strip of paper onto the glue. Press it down. Do the next strip and the next, adding a ribbon where you like. Continue to the end. The last strip of paper may hang over the edge of the cardboard. That is fine. Press all of them down firmly and leave to dry. The long ends of the strips are draped over both sides of the cardboard.

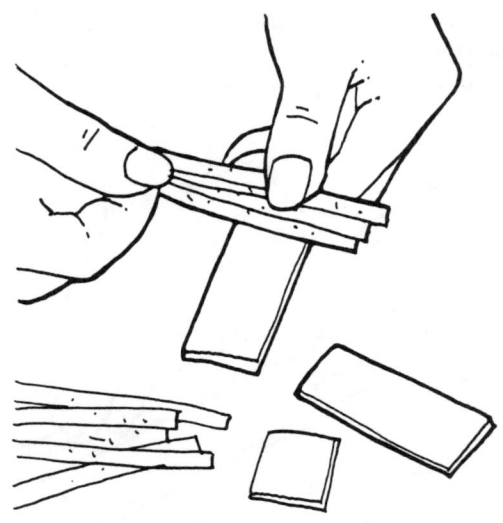

7 Paint a coat of PVA glue on the front of the piece, going a little beyond the cardboard edge. This gives the paper strength and makes it easier to cut the edges cleanly. Leave to dry completely. After you get the hang of it you can work on three or four pieces at once.

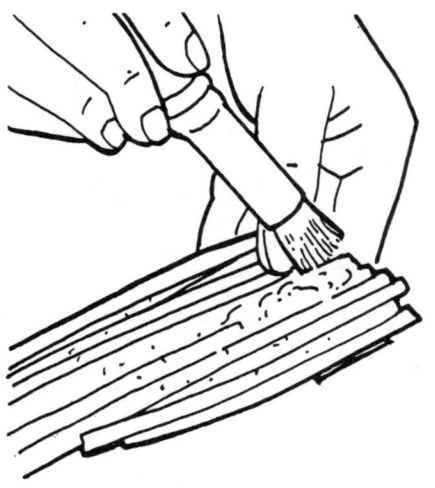

8 When the glue is dry, place the piece face down on the cutting mat. Line up the ruler with the edge of the cardboard. Press the ruler down firmly to hold the cardboard in place. Using the craft knife with a new blade, trim the long ends of the strips of paper flush with the edge of the cardboard.

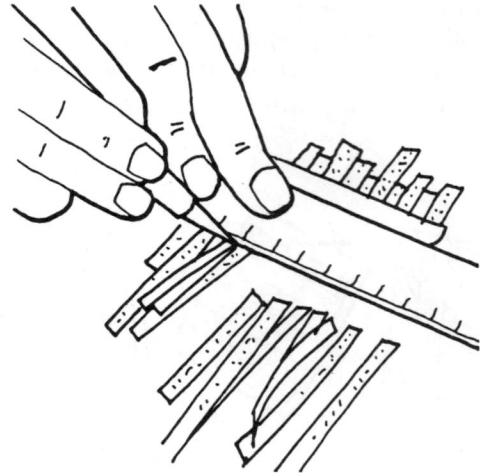

9 Holding it with a finger on each side, paint glue along the four edges for strength. Let dry.

10 Paint glue across the whole back of the piece. When the glue is tacky, place the brooch back or earring clip (finding) into position. Leave to dry. You may want an extra dab of glue on the finding to be sure it is well anchored.

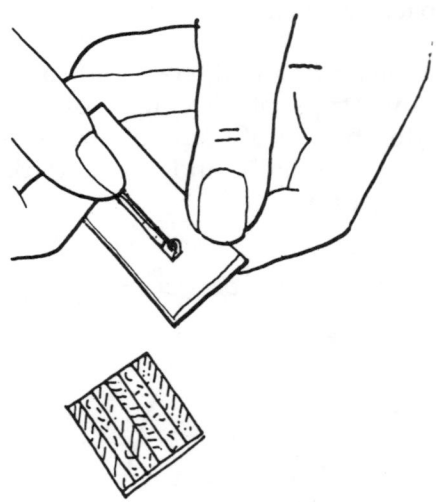

11 The papers may need a second coat of glue across the front, and then you are done! If you are giving it as a gift, attach it to a brightly coloured square of paper and wrap in tissue. It is better than a bought one!

Shell necklace

More jewellery! Try making this pretty shell necklace, shown in the photograph facing page 33. Here, handmade paper shells are strung between beads. The shells look delicate, but they are strong. You can use the same technique to make matching earrings.

Equipment needed
One sheet of heavy handmade paper (must not be embossed); PVA glue, an inexpensive bristle brush, pencil, tracing paper, triangle; a cutting mat, craft knife, scrap newspaper; thread or wire or fishing line to string beads; two small packets of beads and four large beads to match; small empty containers for beads; a barrel closure or hooks; needle nose pliers and crimps (available from bead shops).

1 Trace the fan shape shown with tracing paper and pencil. Cut out shape for fan template.

2 Place the template on the handmade paper and trace it three times in pencil. Remove template. Cut out fan shapes from your handmade paper.

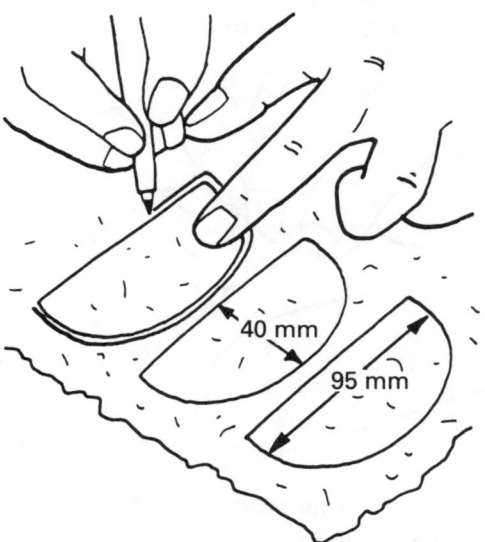

pattern for fan template

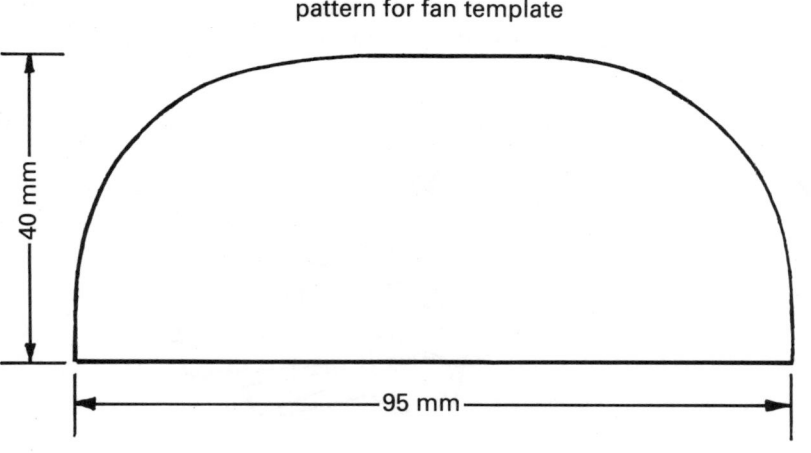

40 mm

95 mm

3 Cut out three strips of handmade paper for loops, 5 mm × 45 mm.

4 Accordion-fold the fan shape as evenly as possible, each fold parallel to the last.

5 Paint glue on one side of each fan shape with bristle brush. Leave to get tacky. Pinch at one end to form the fan shape. Hold or clip with a clothes peg until completely dry. Be patient.

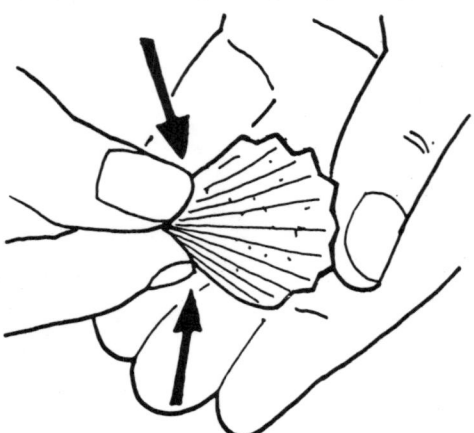

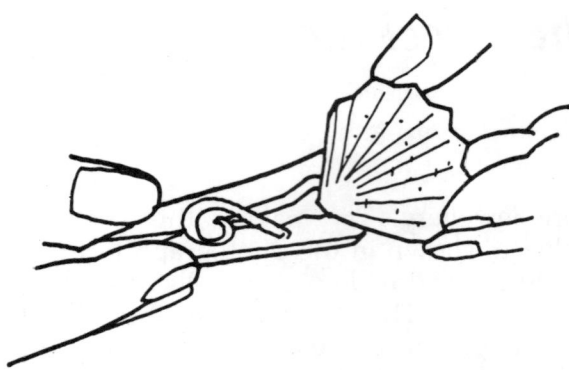

6 Paint the other side of the fans with glue. Leave to dry. This strengthens and helps protect the paper. A second coat may be needed on each side if paper is absorbent.

7 With a new sharp blade, trim the base of the folded fan even, if necessary.

8 Paint glue on one side of all three strips. Let dry. Paint the other side of the strip with glue. Bend strips and glue in a loop.

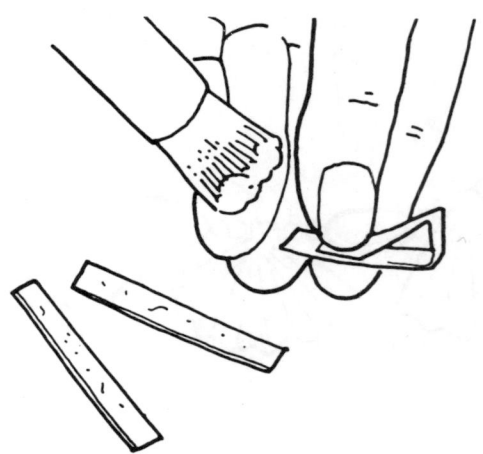

9 Mark the position of the loops on the fans. Glue one side of the loops and one side of the pinched end of the fans. Allow to get tacky. Press loops in position and leave to dry.

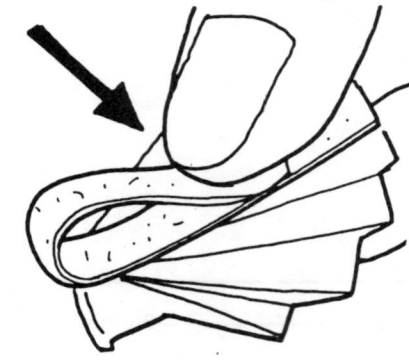

10 Choose the length you want for your necklace (mine is 45 cm). Leave 1 cm extra at each end. Cut the thread to this length.

11 Using crimp and pliers, put the barrel clasp on one end of the thread.

12 Now you need to see how many beads fit on each side of the fans to make them centred. Place the three fans on the table, in an arc, leaving space between them for a few beads. Fold the thread in half to find its centre. Hold this spot over the middle fan.

13 Note how much space the fans take along the thread. Mark this on the thread with a pen.

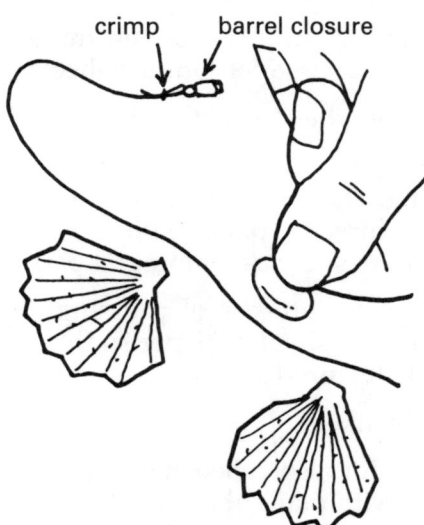

14 String the small beads onto your thread to a point just before this mark.

15 String a large bead, two small beads and the first fan.

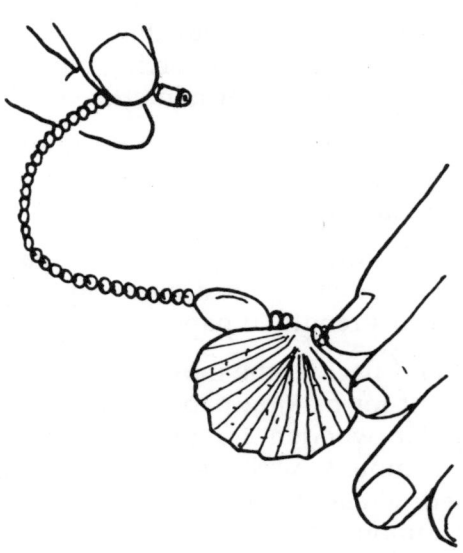

16 String two more small beads, a large bead, two more small beads and the second fan. This is the centre.

17 String two small beads, one large, two small beads and the third fan.

18 String two small beads, and one large.

19 Count how many beads are between the clasp and the first large bead on the other side. Add this many more small beads to reach the other end of the necklace.

20 Put on the second side of the clasp, using the crimp and pliers.

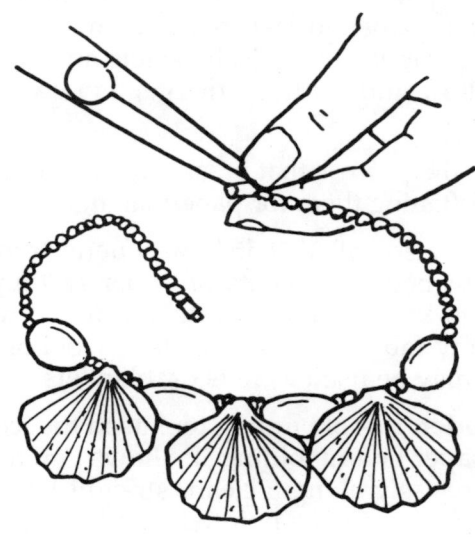

21 You are done. You have a new fashion accessory! Wear it and brag!

22 To make matching earrings, simply make two more shells and glue earring clips onto the backs instead of loops.

Glossary

Acid-free paper: only of concern to those who want their paper to last intact for many years. Acid-free paper is chemically stable and will not turn yellow and brittle with age, as newspaper does.

Beating: the process that breaks up and separates fibres, softening them for papermaking.

Blankets: also called 'felts'. A general term for fabric put between sheets of paper as they are formed to keep them separate and to aid drainage. Many fabrics, such as cotton, wool or synthetics, may be used as felts or 'blankets'.

Bone folder: a bookbinding tool used for scoring heavy paper before folding. It allows you to fold paper precisely along a clean, straight line. The handle of a spoon or a pointed wooden tool used in ceramics works equally well.

Casting paper: processes to shape paper into three-dimensional forms.

Caustic soda: also called soda ash. An alkali added to water, that helps to break down plant fibres when boiling them. Wood ash is similar, though weaker. Caustic is added to the water used in the boiling. It needs to be handled with extreme caution. It must not come into contact with exposed skin, eyes, etc. If it does, flush the affected area liberally with water and see a doctor.

Colourants: various additives used to colour paper.

Cotton linters: a bright white pulp, ideal for casting. It comes from the cotton seed and consists of the shorter fibres left behind when the longer fibres are used for cotton fabric.

Couching: the process of transferring a newly formed sheet of paper from the screen of the mould to the wet blankets. Pronounced COO-ching, from the French, *coucher*, to lie down.

Craft knife: a lightweight hobby knife with a sharp, changeable blade.

Deckle: the rectangular wooden frame that fits over the mould, used for forming sheets of paper.

Deckle edge: the distinctive irregular edge of handmade paper.

Embedding: the process of forming sheets of paper with threads, photos, images, etc., incorporated in the sheet as an integral part.

Embossing: the process of pressing a textured object against a sheet of paper so that the paper takes on its textured surface.

Felts: see blankets.

Formation aid: also called mucilage. Formation aid is used with plant fibre pulps. It thickens the pulp and water mixture and slows down drainage from the mould, thus giving you time to distribute the fibres evenly across the mould when forming sheets.

G clamps: metal screw clamps used to clamp the two boards together with the post of paper between them to press out the water. Pressing strengthens the paper by forcing out the water, allowing the fibres to form interlocking bonds.

Kissing it back: a technique to return pulp from the mould and deckle to the vat when a mistake has been made in forming the sheet.

Methyl cellulose: wallpaper paste. A paste made up from a powder, used as a paper glue, for sizing or to strengthen paper.

Mould and deckle: the most important piece of equipment for making paper. It consists of two rectangular wooden frames that fit together, one (the mould) with woven metal screening stretched across it. Stainless steel screening is most common.

Mucilage: see formation aid.

Plant fibre: paper can be made from cotton or linen rags, wood pulp or many plant fibres. The plants are cut into short lengths, retted, boiled, beaten and blended to be prepared.

Post: a stack of newly formed sheets of paper with felts or blankets in between them.

Presses: equipment used to exert physical force on paper to squeeze out the water from new sheets.

Pulp: any fibre that has been broken down and is ready to be made into paper.

Pulp painting: a technique of creating an image by squirting coloured pulps from squeezable plastic sauce bottles or by working with your hands.

Retting: the process of leaving plant fibres to rot to begin breaking down the non-cellulose parts of the plant before boiling. The fibre is moistened and left in the open air, allowing bacteria in. This is best done in the backyard as the smells are not pleasant.

Size: a weak glue. Sizing is necessary when papers are to be used for writing or painting. It strengthens the paper and reduces its absorbency, preventing paints and inks bleeding into it.

Vat: a large rectangular basin to hold the water and paper pulp mix.

Watermark: a patterned area of paper, often the logo or initials of the papermaker, that is more translucent than the rest of the sheet. It is best seen when paper is held up to the light.

Resources

Organisations for papermakers

NEW SOUTH WALES

Papermakers of New South Wales
62 Pennant Avenue
Denistone East, NSW 2112
(02) 809 7552

QUEENSLAND

Papermakers of Queensland
Paul and Ria Somogyi
72 Spence Street
Mt Gravatt, Qld 4122
(07) 849 5720

VICTORIA

Papermakers of Victoria
for newsletter, advice, workshops
Valda Quick, Secretary
14 Dalmor Avenue
Mitcham Vic 3132
(03) 874 4050
or
Helen McPherson, President
PO Box 18
Eltham Vic 3095
(03) 523 0170

WESTERN AUSTRALIA

Geraldton Papermakers
321 Marine Terrace
Geraldton WA 6530
(099) 21 7005

Papermakers Guild of Western
Australia
Gladys Dove
37 Denny Way
Alfred Cove WA 6154
(09) 330 4102

THE NETHERLANDS

International Association of Hand
Papermakers and Paper Artists
Pat Gentenaar-Torley
Sir W. Churchilllaan 1009
2286 AD Rijswijk
The Netherlands

Workshops

ACT

Crafts Council of the ACT
1 Aspinal Street
Watson ACT 2602
(062) 41 2373

NEW SOUTH WALES

Crafts Council of Australia
1st Floor, 100 George Street
The Rocks, Sydney NSW 2000
(02) 241 1701

Crafts Council of NSW
The Rocks, Sydney NSW 2000
(02) 27 9126

Colleen Pinkerton
99 Morgan Street
Merewether NSW 2291
(049) 63 2158

Primrose Park Art & Craft Centre
PO Box 152
Cremorne NSW 2090
Workshops, moulds and deckles,
studio for rent

NORTHERN TERRITORY

Crafts Council of the Northern
Territory
PO Box 1479
Darwin NT 5794
(089) 81 6615
or
Barbara Butten
PO Box 85
Alice Springs NT 0871
(089) 52 4417

Winsome Jobling
38 Wells Street
Ludmilla NT 0820
(089) 22 1622

Jennette Kendall
PO Box 941
Alice Springs NT 0871
(089) 52 5703

Jenny Maddern
PO Box 2091
Katherine NT 0851
(089) 72 3595

QUEENSLAND

Crafts Council of Queensland
School of Arts Building
166 Ann Street
Brisbane Qld 4000
(07) 229 2661

Christine Ballinger
Flaxton Mill Road
Flaxton Mill Qld 4560
(074) 457 317

Marion Gaemers
23 Seventh Street
Townsville Qld 4810
(077) 71 6803

Lynn Kaddatz
PO Box 3283
North Mackay Qld 4740
(079) 55 1430

Patricia Laing
250 Mortimer Road
Acacia Ridge Qld 4110
(07) 277 3865

McGregor Summer School
PO Box 100
Toowoomba Qld 4350
(076) 32 1422

Bill Wim
85 Lindsay Street
Toowoomba Qld 4350
(076) 38 2594

Meg Woods
Also sells moulds and deckles
24 Elourera Drive
Yandina Qld 4561
(074) 46 7842

SOUTH AUSTRALIA

Crafts Council of South Australia
169 Payneham Road
St Peters SA 5069
(08) 363 0383

Ruth Creedy and Heather McDonald
PO Box 248
Bel Air SA 5052
(08) 271 4802

University of South Australia
Ian Arcus, Textile Dept
Holbrooks Road
Underdale SA 5032
(08) 302 6611

TASMANIA

Crafts Council of Tasmania
Peacock Building
77 Salamanca Place
Hobart Tas 7000
(002) 23 5622

Tasmanian School of Art
Penny Carey-Wells
GPO Box 252C
Hobart Tas 7001

VICTORIA

Crafts Council of Victoria
7 Blackwood Street
North Melbourne Vic 3051
(03) 329 0611

Papermakers of Victoria
See listing above under 'Organisations
for papermakers'
Provides detailed list of teachers and
workshops in Victoria.

WESTERN AUSTRALIA

Crafts Council of Western Australia
GPO Box D178
Perth WA 6001
(09) 325 2799

Jo Bunker
184 Shenton Street
Geraldton WA 6530
(099) 21 8165
(099) 21 7005

Gretchen Forrest
Mouse and Butterfly Studio
75 Beach Street
Bicton WA 6157
(09) 339 2732

Fremantle Arts Centre
1 Finnerty Street
Fremantle WA 6160
(09) 335 8244

Lois Prosser
49 Nutbush Ave
Falcon WA 6210
(09) 582 2452

Sally Read
Lot 14 Hawter Street
Mullayup WA 6252
(097) 64 1106

Peter Thompson
74 Attfield Street
Fremantle WA 6160
(09) 335 2165

Supplies and equipment

NEW SOUTH WALES

Fine Art Papers
Cotton linters
108 Johnston Lane
Annandale NSW 2068
(02) 660 6854

QUEENSLAND

Fred Nichols
1139 Waterworks Road
The Gap Qld 4061
(07) 300 4785

VICTORIA

Peter Zerbe
Papermaking Equipment
5 Dunsterville Street
Sandringham, Vic 3191
(03) 598 6076

WESTERN AUSTRALIA

Art Papers and Supplies
243 Stirling Hwy
Claremont WA 6010
(09) 384 6035

Creative Hot Shop
Prepared plant fibre pulps
108 Beaufort Street
Perth WA 6000
Ph (09) 328 5437

UNITED STATES

Carriage House Paper
A source for everything
Donna Koretsky & Elaine Koretsky
PO Box 197
North Hatfield, MA
01066 USA
Phone/Fax 00111 413 247 5668

Books and magazines

Barrett, Timothy, *Japanese Papermaking
— Traditions, Tools, and Techniques*,
John Weatherill, New York, 1983

Bell, Lilian, *Plant Fibres for
Papermaking*, Liliaceae Press,
McMinnville, Oregon, 1981

*The Art and Craft
of Papermaking
by Sophie Dawson*
Simon & Schuster,
London, 1992

Heller, Jules, *Papermaking*, Watson-
Guptill, New York, 1978

Hunter, Dard, *Papermaking, the History
and Technique of an Ancient Craft*, Dover
Publications, New York, 1947

Ikegami, Kojiro, *Japanese Bookbinding*,
John Weatherill, New York, 1990

Koretsky, Elaine, *Color for the Hand
Papermaker*, Carriage House Press,
Brookline, MA, 1982
   Available from Carriage House
Paper, it is the only book on this
subject.

Shannon, Faith, *Paper Pleasures*,
Angus and Robertson, Sydney, 1987

Studley, Vance, *The Art and Craft of
Handmade Paper*, Dover Publications,
New York, 1990

Toale, Bernard, *The Art of Papermaking*,
Davis Publications, Worcester, MA,
1983

Textile Fibre Forum
Australian Forum for Textile Arts
Sturt Crafts Centre
PO Box 192
Mittagong NSW 2575
(048) 60 2085

Craft Arts Magazine
PO Box 363
Neutral Bay NSW 2089
(02) 908 4797

Index